Three Minutes a Day

VOLUME 42

Other Christopher Books in Print

Father James Keller's
You Can Change the World
Anniversary Edition

and other volumes in the
Three Minutes a Day
series

THREE MINUTES A DAY
VOLUME 42

Dennis Heaney
President, The Christophers

Stephanie Raha
Editor-in-Chief

Margaret O'Connell
Senior Research Editor

Staff Contributing Editors
Lisa Mantineo
Nicholas Monteleone
Anna Marie Tripodi

Contributors
Joan Bromfield
Karen Hazel Radenbaugh
Monica Ann Yehle-Glick

Contributing Interns
Kaitlyn Coppolo
Anton Djamoos
Kenneth Frank
Rebecca Kelleher
Rute Oliveira

The Christophers
5 Hanover Square, 11th Floor
New York, NY 10004

"Teacher," he said, "what must I do to inherit eternal life?" He said to him, "What is written in the law? What do you read there?" (The lawyer) answered, "You shall love the Lord your God with all your heart, and with all your soul, and with all your strength, and with all your mind; and your neighbor as yourself." And (Jesus) said to him, "You have given the right answer; do this, and you will live."

LUKE 10:25-28

Introduction

I once offered someone a copy of *Three Minutes a Day* and was startled by the response: "Thanks but no thanks. I don't have time to read it. My days are too busy and I simply can't add any more to them!"

Imagine my surprise to hear that there's not even three minutes in the day to pause, read and reflect. Still, I commiserate. Some days I'm so overscheduled I don't "stop and smell the roses" either.

Spending time each morning with *Three Minutes a Day* is my way of finding a dose of tranquility to offset being overwhelmed by demands. This book helps me focus–not on meetings and "To Do" lists, but rather on the blessings God has given me. I thank God and ask Him to help me remember that these gifts–family, friends, health and so on–are my priorities, not how much I can get done each day.

My prayer for you is that each day you find tranquility and hope in *Three Minutes a Day.* If you do, we've fulfilled our purpose.

Peace!

Dennis Heaney
President, The Christophers

Resolve on Your Resolutions

How good are you at keeping your New Year's resolutions? The fact is that most people start off with a bang—and then give up when they meet setbacks.

Here are a few ideas from Alex Ferreyra writing in *Positive Thinking* that could help you meet your goals:

- Start early. Good intentions are not enough. Plan how you will achieve your goal.
- Keep it real. Changing habits takes time. Don't make your goal so big that it overwhelms you and your chance for success.
- Be specific. Instead of resolving to lose weight, exercise or whatever, target some specific goals.
- Buddy up. Have someone you can talk with about your mutual efforts.
- Go for something new. If one method doesn't work for you, try another tack.
- Write what you "sow." Keep a journal of all your efforts.

Remember to be patient with yourself—and keep trying.

**Endure everything with patience.
(Colossians 1:11)**

Holy Spirit, guide my attempts to live a healthier, more positive life.

"Here a Patch, There a Patch"

There's something special about turning a hobby into a heartfelt mission of hope. After swapping designs and patterns, long-time knitters Ann Shayne and Kay Gardiner decided to turn their love of knitting into a crusade for charity anyone could enjoy—online.

By posting a request for hand-knit patches on their knitting "blog," the two women were able to create 25 blankets for Afghans for Afghans, a group that sends hand-knit items to those in need in Afghanistan. As Gardiner puts it, "There's something meaningful about people taking on a project together."

That was just the beginning. Inspired by Shayne and Gardiner, other knitters followed their lead in gathering hand-knit items for charities. Thousands have donated their time, knitting, and heartfelt creations to those in need.

Don't keep your good ideas to yourself. Spread the good word and the good deeds.

Do not avert your eyes from the needy. (Sirach 4:5)

May we use the gifts with which we have been blessed to create a positive change in our needy world, Sweet Jesus.

Better Nutrition in Honduras

Vicky Alvarado was tired of seeing malnourished children in her native Honduras. In some areas, 70 percent of residents were undernourished. The problem wasn't money—only two percent of families could not afford to eat daily. The problem was buying and eating the most nutritious foods.

Alvarado, who has a master's degree in nutrition, teamed up with the Honduran Secretary of Health to teach people about hygiene, meal planning and food preparation. Instructors traveled to villages throughout Honduras and the local mothers turned out to learn how to help their families. Statistics from weigh-ins and measurements of children showed that over time they grew healthier.

Alvarado knew immediate action was necessary. She had the tools to help and she didn't stop until people were helped.

One person with a desire to succeed can definitely make a difference for the better. Decide how you can help.

The good person brings good things out of a good treasure. (Matthew 12:35)

Inspire professionals to use their skills for the benefit of the all, but especially those who are poor, sick or powerless, Holy Spirit.

Instead of Worrying...

How do you approach the difficulties in your life—with thought or with worry? They're not the same and your choice will make a huge difference to you.

Here's what writer Harold B. Walker says:

"You can think about your problems or you can worry about them, and there is a vast difference between the two.

"Worry is thinking that has turned toxic. Thinking works its way through problems to conclusions and decisions; worry leaves you in a state of tensely suspended animation.

"When you worry, you go over the same ground endlessly and come out the same place you started. Thinking makes progress from one place to another; worry remains static.

"The problem of life is to change worry into thinking and anxiety into creative action."

Make the effort to think things through and then to make the best choices that you can.

He will cover you with His pinions, and under His wings you will find refuge; His faithfulness is a shield and buckler. (Psalm 91:4)

Help me to rely on You, Divine Lord. Guide my thoughts and actions each day of my life.

Making a Landfill Beautiful

Fresh Kills landfill on Staten Island in New York City consists of four 225-foot high mounds, on about 3.5 square miles of land. It's one of the few manmade things, aside from China's Great Wall, that can be seen from outer space.

Staten Islanders wanted the landfill closed for many years because of the smell and risk of disease that came with the garbage. Fresh Kills closed in March, 2001, but reopened for debris from the World Trade Center before closing again.

Professor Steven Handel, director of the Center for Urban Restoration Ecology, is working with the soil and believes that in time the landfill will again have meadows, forests, and marshes; the garbage contained under a plastic or heavy clay cap.

Henry David Thoreau wrote, "In wilderness is the preservation of the world." We can preserve and restore God's good earth. Recycle. Compost. Live simply.

The wilderness and the dry land shall be glad, the desert shall rejoice and blossom.
(Isaiah 35:1)

Compassionate Creator, remind us that we need wilderness here on this amazing planet of Yours—and ours.

Meet La Befana

In Matthew's gospel, we read about three wise men who traveled west, probably out of Mesopotamia (today's Iran and Iraq), following a star which heralded a king's birth.

According to legend, these Magi stopped at a little house for directions. A wizened old woman, broom in hand, opened the door. No, she did not know the One they sought. No, she did not know the way. And no, she could not join them for she had too much work. The Magi left.

Regretting her decision, she went searching for them and for the Infant-King, but could find neither.

Italians remember her as La Befana. And down the centuries on Epiphany Eve, she still sets out to find the Infant-King. During her search she leaves treats in each good child's stocking (a lump of coal in the naughty ones').

Search for that same Infant-King, Son of God and Son of Man. When you find Him, hug Him tightly to your heart.

There, ahead of them, went the star that they had seen at its rising, until it stopped over the place where the Child was. (Matthew 2:9)

Infant-King, help us find You.

Man's — and Woman's — Best Friend

Sheila Kohler favored cats over dogs. But when she found herself the mother of a blended family, she thought that a puppy might help her two new stepsons warm up to her.

The idea worked, though slowly. From the moment she and her two boys visited the animal shelter to search for the perfect puppy, an intangible, but real bond began forming.

She found herself walking and caring for the family's new companion. Over the next few years, the dog served to bring a step-mom and her stepsons closer.

Ten years after his adoption, Kohler's dog needed surgery. The self-proclaimed "cat person" couldn't hold back her tears, and found a kindred spirit in her youngest stepson, now a teenager.

Blended families face unique challenges. How can you support those who are starting anew in the face of difficulties? A kind word and vote of confidence can make all the difference.

Thus says the Lord of hosts...show kindness and mercy to one another...and do not devise evil... against one another. (Zechariah 7:9,10)

God in Heaven, bless the efforts of all families to be united.

Neighbors Help Neighbors

How can a community help neighbors in trouble? Let's look at the ways that parishioners at St. Philomena's in Chicago provide food and clothes to hundreds of needy people thanks to the generosity of many.

- Their food pantry serves an average of 400 people twice a week, offering food such as meat, rice, canned and baked goods.

- Individuals collect, bag and distribute groceries.

- People prune their closets to provide clothing for adults and children.

- Neighbors take pledges for each mile walked in the annual five-mile "Hunger Walk" along Lake Michigan.

In communities small and large across the country, neighbors help neighbors. Could people in your village, town, or city use your help today?

Am I my brother's keeper? (Genesis 4:9)

Never let us forget, Abba, that our lives are woven together in mutual responsibility for each other, for all Your creatures and for earth itself.

75-Year-Old Twins Accept Challenge

"What can two 75-year-old ladies like us do?" Marjorie Maitland asked her sister Marguerite. Their minister had challenged the twins and other students in a discipleship class to do something to help the community.

After researching ideas, the sisters decided to start a fund, which would reward youngsters in their school district who remained drug free through high school graduation.

"We took donations, applied for grants, and had bake sales. We even got in touch with alumni dating all the way back to 1915," Maitland notes. "Marge and I are now 90 years old, and the project is going strong. We've got it set up so that it will go on even after we're gone."

The sisters accepted their minister's challenge and learned that one person can make a difference. "Well, two in this case," says Marguerite Maitland.

They're leaving an admirable legacy we could all emulate.

Encourage the fainthearted, help the weak. (1 Thessalonians 5:14)

Who needs whatever encouragement I can provide, Good Shepherd?

A New Revolution in China?

China is experiencing a spiritual resurgence. A poll recognized by the official Communist paper says more than 31 percent of those over 16 years of age call themselves religious. That's about 300 million people.

Why? Experts cite the growing gap between rich and poor and various social crises. "People feel troubled and wonder how issues will be resolved. They think, 'I want something to rely upon,'" says Liu Zhongyu, a professor at East China Normal University which conducted the survey.

China allows five sanctioned, although controlled, religions: Buddhism, Taoism, Islam, Catholicism and Protestantism.

One 74-year-old man, who spent seven years in prisons and labor camps for his Catholic beliefs, says, "We don't hate anyone and I have no regrets. One must try not to focus on the hardships you endure for faith."

Let's be grateful for both our faith and the freedom to practice it.

Faith is the assurance of things hoped for, the conviction of things not seen. ...By faith we understand that...what is seen was made from things that are not visible. (Hebrews 11:1,3)

Look with mercy on all who long to grow in faith, hope and love, God.

When a Little Means a Lot

Sometimes all you need is a little help. But if you don't get it, you have a big problem. Proponents of micro-philanthropy see it as a small boost that can make a huge difference.

Projects supported by the Archangel Foundation in Texas have included contributing funds to complete a small yet significant day-care-center playground; buying and delivering school uniforms and supplies; providing cash for college textbooks; paying a single mother's utility bill.

The anonymous Texas family that started this nonprofit wasn't wealthy, just comfortable and caring. "We might not have millions," said a spokesperson, "but we might have hundreds that we can put aside (to) help somebody out."

Recipients aren't asked to pay back the one-time donations of money or gifts. Instead they are asked to "pay it forward"—to be aware of a neighbor's need and to help when they can so that today's beneficiaries can become tomorrow's benefactors.

**Be rich in good works, generous.
(1 Timothy 6:18)**

The most obvious way to be generous is to give money; the more costly way is to share time and talents. Help us to be generous in every way, Jesus.

A Marriage of Hearts and Hopes

Married couples know that it can be all too easy to take their spouse for granted. And that can undermine even the best relationship.

Rabbi Zelig Pliskin encourages husbands and wives to pay attention to each other and to their marriage. In his book, *Marriage,* he says, "I once saw this advertisement: 'Make sure you're part of a winning team.' The way to be part of a winning team in marriage is to bring out the best in your spouse.

"Remember to keep your focus on your spouse's strengths and not his or her weaknesses. Remember to believe in the potential of your spouse. Believe that your spouse has untapped wisdom and goodness that both of you can reach. Remember to notice positive changes and to express your appreciation."

We all need to be noticed and appreciated. Make a special effort to help your loved ones to grow into their best selves.

Let love be genuine...love one another with mutual affection; outdo one another in showing honor. (Romans 12:9,10)

Eternal God, show spouses the way to encourage and nurture each other to be the persons You made them to be.

Be Joyful!

In the face of major global problems as well as more personal ones, many people still realize that joy in life is possible and worth cultivating.

Motivational speaker Chris Widener says, "Joy can be yours! Look for it, pursue it and enjoy it!" and offers seven tips:

- Know your unique purpose in life and fulfill it.
- Live purposefully. Set priorities so you can act in accordance with what you know to be your purpose.
- Stretch yourself. Expand your horizons. Don't settle for the status quo.
- Give more than you take. Being generous brings joy to self and others.
- Surprise yourself and others. On occasion, do the unexpected.
- Indulge yourself from time to time.
- Laugh a little. No, a lot!

To this list, add your own personal notes of joy. When problems threaten to overwhelm you, joy is possible.

A joyful heart is life itself and rejoicing lengthens one's life span. (Sirach 30:22)

Creator, please show us how to cultivate joy in our lives.

Triple-Filtered Talk

It's not unusual to find yourself listening to tales about other people. Here's a story about what one man did about it.

In ancient Greece, a man approached a philosopher and asked, "Do you know what I just heard about one of your friends?"

"Before you tell me about my friend, let's filter what you're going to say, first, by truth," said the philosopher. "Are you sure what you're about to say is true?"

"Well, no. I just heard about it," the man replied.

"Now, let's try the filter of goodness. Is the news good?"

"Oh, no, quite to the contrary, it was bad."

"Finally, tell me if the information is useful."

"No, not really."

"So, if what you want to tell me is neither true, nor good, nor even useful, why tell it to me at all," asked the philosopher.

Let all we say be true, good and useful.

**Speak the truth to one another.
(Zechariah 8:16)**

Bless my speech and hearing, Trinity.

"A Very Sweet 16"

Alexa Coughenour gave away all of the gifts that she received for her Sweet 16 birthday party—even though she specifically requested what she wanted on her invitations and got exactly what she asked for. Her request: donations of money and canned goods for the needy in her community.

"I just thought, I'm turning 16 and that's a pretty big thing, and I could do something different to help others," she said.

Her good deed resulted in a $300 check that she donated to the Jubilee Soup Kitchen in Pittsburgh on Martin Luther King Day.

"The best way to honor Dr. King is to have young people become conscious of the needs of the poor, and she's certainly done this," said Sister Liguori Rossner, executive director of the soup kitchen.

We all have the power to help others. How can you make a difference in someone's life today?

I commend to you our sister Phoebe, a deacon of the church at Cenchreae, so that you may welcome her in the Lord. (Romans 16:1-2)

Support women and men in their passion to serve You and Your daughters and sons in need, Holy Spirit.

Faith Making a Difference

"Lucious' faith has taught me that when you pray and put God in your life, there's no limit to what you can do," said Pete Molloy about his friend Lucious Newsom, who is over 90.

A retired Baptist minister turned Catholic, Newsom dreamed of opening "Anna's House" in Indianapolis as a beacon of hope; a place where food, education, medical and dental care are provided. He chose the name Anna in honor of Molloy's young daughter. She helps feed the poor from her wheelchair.

Whenever Newsom helped others, he saw gratitude on their faces and liked the feeling. His spirit inspired others to contribute. "They said, 'I'll pay for the siding. I'll pay for the plumbing. I'll pay for this and that.' It's more than what I hoped for."

Newsom wants to make a positive difference in the lives of those he meets for as long as possible. What a wonderful goal!

Tobit...performed many acts of charity. (Tobit 1:3)

May others' examples inspire me to deeds of charity, Lord of Life.

Seven Habits for Mentors

Mentoring others well takes work. *Ode* magazine listed these habits of highly effective mentors:

Listen. It enables you to learn about the person.

Build a solid relationship. Trust is vital to a successful, long term relationship.

Respect boundaries. Wait until a successful relationship has been formed before asking anything too personal.

Stay sensitive to all differences. Your backgrounds may be very different and the other person may feel some embarrassment.

Provide both support and challenges. Offer constant guidance. Help with problems; don't simply say what to do.

Acknowledge reciprocity. Learn give and take. Sharing serves to strengthen a relationship.

Be realistic. A person may be unresponsive and elusive, but you can help them achieve goals.

Don't forget, all relationships take time to develop.

A generous person will be enriched.
(Proverbs 11:25)

Guide teachers, business people and all who mentor others, Divine Teacher.

Tucson to the Rescue

Linda Rae Smith was having problems with life's daily tasks. Diagnosed with Multiple Sclerosis, she sometimes slurred her words and felt unsteady on her feet. These forced her to retire from teaching—a profession she loved more than anything.

Then her husband suggested that she get a service dog to help her. Tucson, a seven-week-old Golden retriever, became Smith's "stabilizer." Wearing a harness, he aids her steadiness when she walks.

After watching people's positive reactions to Tucson, and his love for children, she decided it was time to reach out to others. The two began volunteering with programs that use service dogs to enrich others' lives. They visit classrooms regularly. Tucson even goes to church with her, giving out toys for special holidays.

One door closed for Smith, but with the help of Tucson, a new one opened. Seek new doors to hope in your own life.

A wide door for effective work has opened to me. (1 Corinthians 16:9)

Thank You, Lord, for the intelligence and calmness of service animals who help the sick and handicapped navigate through life.

Saving a School One Envelope at a Time

Ten-year-old Vicky was thriving at Chicago's St.Paul-Our Lady of Vilna School. She earned straight As and was improving her musical talents. Her mom especially appreciated the school's safety, expansive curriculum and supportive teaching staff.

Not surprisingly, when Vicky heard that the school was struggling financially and was planning to merge with another Catholic school, both she and her mom were devastated.

They quickly joined a volunteer group that was starting an emergency fund-raising campaign, stuffing and sealing what seemed like countless envelopes. Before long, they began to see results. While the effort continues, the school has remained open, thanks to the hope-filled effort of people like Vicky and her mother.

Challenges can be an avenue to self-improvement, achievement and success. Use them to reach your goals.

A woman who fears the Lord is to be praised. Give her a share in the fruit of her hands, and let her works praise her. (Proverbs 31:30-31)

Dear God, help young people have confidence and success in their attempts to do good.

Keeping a Sabbath

An article in *Our Sunday Visitor* newspaper said that "there are no mechanisms in today's society to support your decision to make Sunday a holy day." Here are a few suggestions to reclaim the day as a true Sabbath:

- Have communal, family and individual worship and prayer.
- Make a conscious decision not to go shopping.
- Plan so that weekend chores are mostly completed.
- Gather the family for meals around a table set with a table cloth, napkins, flowers and candles and the good dishes.
- Say a special Sabbath grace before meals.
- Use a crock pot to free Mom or Dad from cooking.
- Include quiet time, outdoor activities, games, cultural events.

Rabbi Abraham Joshua Heschel said an internalized Sabbath was what has preserved Judaism. That's a splendid example for Christians and people of all faiths.

Six days you shall labor and do all your work. But the seventh day is a Sabbath to the Lord...(who) blessed the Sabbath day and consecrated it. (Exodus 20:9-10,11)

Lord of the Sabbath, help us to rest in You.

Second Chances

In 2006, 46 years after he had been expelled, Rev. James Lawson, a leading scholar on civil disobedience and Gandhi's nonviolence, returned to teach at Vanderbilt University. Lawson had been a Methodist divinity student at the Tennessee university when he was expelled for his involvement in lunch counter sit-ins during the civil rights movement.

In the years since, Vanderbilt has apologized to Lawson, bestowed honors on him and finally invited him to teach. Lawson said he never held a grudge against the school and hadn't expected the teaching offer. But he will use his position to share his nonviolent beliefs with a new generation.

"It isn't often that an institution gets the chance to correct a previous error," said one administrator.

We, too, don't always get that second chance. Take the opportunity when you can.

Loose the bonds of injustice. (Isaiah 58:6)

Holy Spirit, to whom do I owe an apology? Show me how to ask forgiveness for my mistakes.

Choosing Life

It's fair to say that Debbie Borza has experienced far more than her fair share of emotional pain. Borza's daughter, Deora Bodley, was the youngest person killed aboard United Flight 93 during the 2001 terrorist attacks on the U.S.

Then, her former husband, Derrill Bodley, Deora's father, died in a motorcycle accident.

Despite the burden of grief that she carries daily, Borza says she has made a conscious decision to look for positive ways to ease her pain.

"Since I'm probably going to spend the rest of my life trying to fill that void, I choose joy and happiness and peace and love," she says. Borza now seeks out people inspired by her daughter's life, encouraging volunteerism in her memory.

Surely those who are able to remain hopeful and faithful in the face of loss will be blessed. Reach out to console the bereaved people in your life.

Those who mourn...will be comforted.
(Matthew 5:4)

Jesus, infuse us with Your everlasting hope.

Wishing Every Day Was Wednesday

Jack Williams enjoyed a near-meteoric rise to fame as a popular TV-news anchor in Boston, a top-tier media market. Then the Phi Beta Kappa scholar and father of six children realized that his fame and success could be put to work for others.

He was concerned about special-needs children in foster care, who, because they were older, had siblings or had physical or mental disabilities, had been passed over for adoption.

Williams' own childhood had been idyllic: "I was loved and adored, and my idea of abuse was not getting any dessert." He believes that every child needs a chance to love and be loved and to succeed.

Williams leveraged his on-air fame to launch "Wednesday's Child," a television feature that spotlights special-needs children waiting to be adopted. In the show's 25-year run, over 500 children have been placed with adoptive families.

Use your talents to help others and to show gratitude for your many blessings.

Be thankful. (Colossians 3:15)

Lord God, remind me that all good comes through You, and only You.

To Become Motivated

You probably have any number of goals you'd like to achieve, if only you could find the motivation: find another job…learn a new language …contribute time and skills to a favorite charity and more.

Lisa Goff wrote in *Good Housekeeping* magazine about four steps that can help boost your motivation:

1. Dream big, but start small. At first, pick easily achievable goals.
2. Find inspiration. Discover why you procrastinate, then work on things that mean the most to you.
3. Renew your focus daily. Try posting your goal in a prominent spot or enlist the support of friends.
4. Reward yourself. Choose something special like a new book—or the time to read it.

You can achieve your goals. Begin today.

Encourage the fainthearted, help the weak, be patient…do good to one another and to all. (1 Thessalonians 5:14,15)

Deliver us from discouragement, Spirit of Fortitude.

In Her Pain She Helped Others

Best-known for her role in the 1980's sitcom *Bosom Buddies,* Wendie Jo Sperber was born to entertain. So when the comedic actress was diagnosed with breast cancer in 1997, she made the best of the life-threatening disease.

Dissatisfied with the institutional feel of support programs for cancer patients, Sperber created the "weSPARK Cancer Support Center" in Sherman Oaks, California. It offers cancer patients everything from jewelry-making classes to holistic treatments, free. She personally organized fund-raising events such as celebrity golf tournaments and variety shows.

Although Wendy Jo Sperber lost her own battle with cancer in 2005, friends at the cancer support center insist her spirit will always be there—helping them help others.

Even difficult times can be made better by sharing our blessings with others.

Kindred and helpers are for a time of trouble. (Sirach 40:24)

Divine Physician, inspire researchers who are looking for the causes and cures for cancer.

Ready For A Change?

According to the AARP, more and more people 50 and older are seeking happiness and fulfillment by changing careers.

"My only regret is that I didn't make the change years ago," said Henry Stewart. He left public relations to pursue his passion as a chef.

Architect Rebecca Armstrong became a nurse. "Architecture has an impact on people's lives, but I wanted a direct connection," she says. "I feel like I am doing exactly what I've wanted to do my entire life."

Jeri Sedlar, co-author of *Don't Retire, Rewire!,* says these changes "shouldn't be taken lightly or acted on impulsively." There are financial, emotional and practical considerations. But there are rewards, too.

Joyce Roche took her talents as a corporate executive into the nonprofit field. "I used to go on vacation to feel reenergized and rejuvenated. Now I feel that way everyday."

With proper planning, you can make change work for you.

Each builder must choose with care how to build. (1 Corinthians 3:10)

Guide the career and retirement decisions of older workers, Eternal Father.

"A Rough in the Diamond"

Diamonds are symbols of wealth, power and luxury. But in Africa, these diamonds cost more than money—they cost lives.

Blood diamonds are gems implicated, through the manner in which they are mined, in serious human rights abuses, child labor, and environmental destruction.

50,000 people have died and 20,000 men, women, and children have lost limbs to machete-wielding rebels who have seized control of Sierra Leone's diamond mines. At the same time, 46 percent of Angola's miners are under the age of 16.

The human rights violations are not only the result of strife in Africa, but also the lack of efforts to stop the trade in these diamonds. A 2004 *Amnesty International* survey found that only 11 percent of U.S. jewelers had a blood diamond policy.

Make informed choices about everything you buy and you can make a real difference.

Let your adornment be the inner self with the lasting beauty of a gentle and quiet spirit. (1 Peter 3:4)

Help us stand up for what is right in what we say, do—and buy, Holy Spirit.

Play Games for Good Health and Fun

Think word games and puzzles are only for kids? Research shows that adults who play Sudoku or Scrabble are improving brain activity and metabolism. Word games are especially important for the elderly because they exercise their brains.

Gary Small writes about other healthy habits in his book, *The Longevity Bible*.

- Sharpen your mind by completing word puzzles.
- Maintain a positive attitude on life.
- Cultivate close relationships with loved ones.
- Promote less stress in your life by doing yoga or meditating.
- Master your surroundings. Become better organized.
- Get fit by doing cardiovascular exercises.
- Eat healthy foods: fruits, vegetables, proteins, whole grains.

Exercise the one and only body and mind you'll ever have.

There is no wealth better than health of body. (Sirach 30:16)

Encourage me to do all I can to be and to stay healthy, Blessed Trinity.

Symbol of Hope

Kentucky Derby winner Barbaro became a symbol of hope for horse lovers and others after his serious injury and valiant, though ultimately futile, struggle to recover.

Barbaro shattered his right hind leg at the start of the 2006 Preakness Stakes. In similar circumstances another horse would have been quickly put down. Given impressive financial resources, commitment, veterinary expertise as well as love Barbaro received the best care available over many months.

William Rhoden, writing in the *New York Times*, said, "Barbaro may provide the model for how far and to what lengths veterinary medicine can go to keep an injured horse from being destroyed."

While we may hope for an injured animal's recovery; a struggling athlete's win; or an underdog's triumph, sometimes the real victory lies in the hope that is given to others.

Hope that is seen is not hope... But if we hope for what we do not see, we wait for it with patience. (Romans 8:24,25)

Compassionate Creator, remind us to treat all animals, our fellow creatures, with respect and care.

Taking One Terrific Taxi

If you think riding in or, worse, driving, a cab in New York City has to be a major hassle, then you haven't met Paul Hintersteiner.

Calling himself "your positive taxi driver," he not only obeys the speed limit, he hops out to open the door for passengers and plays them soothing classical music. First a chef, then a limousine driver, Hintersteiner started driving a cab after 9/11. But he still wears his chauffeur suit and cap and makes a point of handing out thank-you cards to all his fares.

"I want people to leave my car more positive than when they came in." says this New Yorker. He was awarded a Professionalism Award by the Taxi and Limousine Commission.

Each one of us chooses the way we perform on the job. Beyond doing our work competently, we can also do it with *joie de vivre*—a blessing to those around us as well as to ourselves.

Artisan and master artisan...rely on their hands and all are skillful in their own work. Without them no city can be inhabited, and...they maintain the fabric of the world.
(Sirach 38:27,31-32,34)

Enable us find joy in our work and in performing it well, Carpenter from Nazareth.

Singing And Praying Twice

Renee LaReau, a journalist with the *National Catholic Reporter* and former member of the University of Notre Dame Folk Choir, returned to travel with the group for a few weeks.

The choir "relies on the unlikely partnership of pipe organ and guitar, a rich variety of sacred texts, and hymnody from multiple cultures and ethnic groups," LaReau writes.

And because they tour and publish regularly, their repertoire has found its way into parish and campus choirs and hymnals across the country. The choir has performed for Pope John Paul II, Justice Sandra Day O'Connor and Archbishop Desmond Tutu; in Northern Ireland and in American prisons; using Spanish, Latin, Swahili and Gaelic.

If "those who sing pray twice," as St. Augustine said, then these young people are praying a lot and having a joyful time at it.

Sing out with joy in your own life.

Sing to the Lord, bless His name; tell of His salvation from day to day. Declare His glory... His marvelous works. (Psalm 96:2-3)

Thanks, Beloved God, for the glories of the human voice raised in song, especially in praise of You!

Finding Faith in Strength

Time magazine once called Robert Coles, "the most influential living psychiatrist in the United States."

Witnessing firsthand the fight for civil rights in Mississippi taught him more than any college course. What did people, especially the poor, do in the face of extreme hardship? The answer Cole found was faith.

Take Ruby Bridges who was the first African-American child to attend the Franz School in Gentilly, Mississippi. She prayed as she walked through the angry mob, like "Jesus prayed on the Cross."

Similar stories fill the pages of Coles' *Children of Crisis: A Study of Courage and Fear.* These validated Coles' conclusion that "nothing I have discovered about the makeup of human beings contradicts in any way what I learn from the Hebrew prophets and from Jesus and the lives of those He touched."

The Scriptures remind us that in good and bad times, the love of God is always with us.

My steadfast love shall not depart from you, and My covenant of peace shall not be removed, says the Lord, who has compassion on you. (Isaiah 54:10)

Master, abide with me. Share Your strength.

A Healing Visit

Suitcases heavy with medicine and supplies, 24 doctors, nurses and dentists, an optometrist and others traveled from the United States to El Salvador for a week one recent February.

The trip, organized by the Episcopal Diocese of Central New York, took the team to several villages, bringing medical services to adults and children in areas without access to health care.

Besides sharing their skills and concern with their new El Salvadoran friends, each team member promised, on returning to home, to tell about the great need for medical and dental care in El Salvador. Telling that story, all believed, would help ensure that such efforts would continue.

Trying to solve a problem alone can be difficult–and lonely. But when we share it's amazing the healing help others can–and will–provide.

Bear one another's burdens. (Galatians 6:2)

I pray for Your assistance this day, Creator. In all I do and say today may I live Your will.

Doctor Dog

Love is a two-way street. That's certainly true when it comes to owners and their companion animals.

An American Animal Association survey found that three-quarters of pet owners cite affection as their pet's most endearing quality. Research from Stanford University shows that the love is returned, suggesting that our altruistic behavior makes caring for pets beneficial.

Marivic Dizon from Stanford reports that adults and children who feel empathy towards their pets manifest stronger feelings of empathy toward other people.

In another study, elderly persons who had a pet felt better—mentally and physically—than their pet-less counterparts.

"There are great benefits to appreciating and nurturing animals," concludes Dizon, "and they are good for the animals as well as for us."

Giving and receiving love makes the world go round the way it should.

If I...do not have love, I am a noisy gong or a clanging cymbal. ...I am nothing. ...I gain nothing. (1 Corinthians 13:1,2,3)

What joy I find in experiencing Your great love directly and through other people and creatures, Loving Lord!

"Daddy, I Have No Idea"

Just how far does a father's love stretch? The answer: from his own son to 120 eighth-graders.

When Brian Harvey, a middle-school technology teacher in North Carolina, was called for active duty in Iraq, the fate of his students' education was in jeopardy.

"What are they going to do about your class?" asked Brian's father, Boyce Harvey.

"Daddy, I have no idea," his son answered.

That's when Boyce Harvey found the answer. Though he'd never wanted to teach middle-school before, he retired from his job as a federal soil expert and, with the school's blessing, he took over his son's class. By the next year, he had his teaching license.

Now, with Brian Harvey back from Iraq, Boyce Harvey has found a permanent place as a middle-school teacher to his extended family of kids. And father, son, and students are all doing just fine.

Stay open to new opportunities.

He who teaches his son...will glory in him among his friends. (Sirach 30:3)

May the answers we seek come when they are needed most, Holy Wisdom.

To Save Our Earth...Creatively

Biologist and environmentalist John Todd has created "eco-machines" which use nature, not toxic chemicals, to convert waste water into pure water. There's one in South Burlington, Vermont, which is open to visitors.

Eighteen interconnected steel tanks hold ceiling-grazing reeds, banana plants, ginger, calla lilies and water hyacinths; Japanese Koi and native bait fish; and bottom-dwelling freshwater clams and mussels. Each day this huge "eco-machine" transforms 80,000 gallons of waste water—sewerage—into clean water.

Amory Lovins of the Rocky Mountain Institute says, "Todd and his colleagues have transformed our view of wastewater from a noxious nuisance–to be (treated) with poisons to a resource."

How do you change environmental problems into potential? Begin with those breakfast coffee grounds, eggshells and banana skins. Composted, they'll become next year's garden soil.

Make concern for our world a way of life.

It is required of stewards that they be found trustworthy. (1 Corinthians 4:2)

God, inspire and encourage our efforts to be responsible stewards of Creation.

Bring God Into Your Life

Do you have days when you need someone to talk with? Making your relationship with God a greater part of your life can help. Kathy Trocolli, author of *Live Like You Mean It,* has these suggestions:

- Put aside that consuming "to do" list and try to simply be: be still, be willing, be patient.
- Talk to God, the One who knows you best, frequently and in your own language
- Ask what your attitude and face say to others— are you feast or famine for another's soul?
- Ask God to reveal Himself in who you are now, without regard to your personal agenda.

Walk with God daily. Then your life will be a sweet adventure.

I will walk among you, and will be your God, and you shall be My people. I am...God who brought you out of...Egypt...and made you walk erect. (Leviticus 26:12-13)

Merciful Savior, help us, You and me, to walk together every day, all day.

A Penny for Your Prayers?

Kathy Grooms' son was dating a girl whom Grooms felt "was all wrong for him." She had tried reasoning and pleading, but he stood firm.

Then Grooms remembered a woman who, impatient for an answer to her prayer, put every penny she found into a coffee cup. The pennies, she said, were reminders that God was listening to her and would answer her prayer in His time.

Grooms began doing the same thing. As she filled up her coin cup, she would pray, "Please, God, change Caleb's mind."

In time, Grooms began to get to know her son's girlfriend. She discovered that the girl treated her son well and brought out his good qualities. As the cup filled with pennies, Grooms realized that God had, indeed, changed someone's mind–hers!

Tough situations help us see that God's plan for our lives is infinitely more interesting, fulfilling and joyful than anything we can think of ourselves.

A thousand years in Your sight are like yesterday when it is past, or like a watch in the night. (Psalm 90:4)

Give me the patience and perseverance to live into Your will for me, Father God.

Radio Offers Comfort, Inspiration

Ada Ricci is a widow whose poor health confines her to her New York home. But thanks to "Radio Maria," Ricci can be inspired, comforted and even hear Mass in her native Italian. "It is a blessing from God," she says.

Radio Maria is a loose-knit, growing family of stations now numbering about 50 around the world; in North America that includes Toronto, Canada; Guadalajara, Mexico; as well as Houston and New York City. Much of the programming is in Italian and Spanish.

Eventually, Radio Maria would like to reach out to more immigrants' children, and to broadcast in English on a more easily accessible AM or FM frequency. Currently, a special radio unit must be used.

Encourage all communicators to reach out to people of all backgrounds with worthwhile, spiritual and cultural programming.

Listen to advice and accept instruction, that you may gain wisdom for the future. (Proverbs 19:20)

Bless those in the media who reach out to Your people with life-enhancing work, Abba.

Teen Saves Town Market

When the only grocery store in Truman, Minnesota, (population 1,200) closed in 2006, folks worried about making it to the nearest one 12 miles away–especially during the winter.

And that's when high school senior Nick Graham stepped in. Believing that "a town can't survive without a grocery store," he convinced the town's economic development board to buy the building and lease it to him. Then he invested his savings of $10,000, earned from farm and construction jobs, in the Main Street Market.

He puts in 70 hour weeks and, along with three employees, keeps the place going while the grateful town keeps shopping. His economics teacher says, "The great thing is that, for Nick, it's not about Nick. It's about Truman. He doesn't want the town to die."

Young people have so much to offer. Encourage those in your life to help others.

They found Him in the temple, sitting among the teachers, listening to them and asking them questions. And all who heard Him were amazed. (Luke 2:46-47)

Spirit of Counsel, grant people of all ages the desire to serve their neighbors.

On the Seventh Day, We Rested

When Lynne Baab and her husband who are Christian moved to Tel Aviv, Israel, they found that everything closed from sunset Friday to sunset Saturday in observance of the Sabbath.

At first they struggled to fill the time. But after a while they decided to relax and enjoy the day. They read, walked and talked. She wrote long letters, while he went bird-watching.

"Sometimes we prayed together," Baab explained. "We simply slowed down. We rested in God's love and experienced His grace."

This couple kept the Sabbath slow and work-free even after they returned to the United States. "It remains a day to rest in God's goodness," said Baab who went on to write a book called *Sabbath Keeping*.

Every one of us needs time to slow down the pace—and to enjoy family and friends, or just time alone. What better day than the Sabbath—the day on which God Himself rested.

God...rested on the seventh day from all the work that He had done. So God blessed the seventh day. (Genesis 2:2-3)

Blessed are You, O Lord our God, who has commanded us to observe a weekly Sabbath of rest.

Facing Up to Feelings

When you're striving to succeed in any field of endeavor, it's normal to occasionally feel afraid of the unknown or, alternatively, a loss of enthusiasm.

Janet Guthrie, the first woman sports car driver to qualify and race in the Indianapolis 500, learned to overcome those obstacles. In *Leadership* magazine, she's quoted as saying about fear, "So you're scared. So? Go ahead, let yourself feel scared for a while. Let it out in the open."

As far as sometimes feeling a lack of enthusiasm for the job at hand, Guthrie says, "I must find the space in my mind where there's joy in putting the car through the turns. I've been there before."

We've all been there. First, we need to understand that our emotions are genuine, but temporary. Then we need to acknowledge and deal with them. Only then can we go on to do whatever we need to do to achieve our goals.

Human success is in the hand of the Lord. (Sirach 10:5)

Eternal God, grant me Your strength this day to do all You ask of me.

Lincoln: Leader and Communicator

Great leaders are almost always outstanding communicators. That's certainly true of the sixteenth president of the United States.

In his book, *Lincoln on Leadership,* Donald Phillips states that Abraham Lincoln "learned to express himself and demonstrate to others his beliefs and thoughts. Most importantly, he refined his ability to persuade, direct, and motivate people. ...In fact, he so dramatically increased his ability to speak and write that he is today regarded as a model for poetic and artistic expression."

This is how Lincoln himself described his abilities: "I could not sleep when I got on a hunt for an idea, until I had caught it; and when I thought I had got it, I was not satisfied until I had repeated it over and over again, until I had put it in language plain enough as I thought, for any boy I knew to comprehend."

Make an effort to use language well. It's a gift that will benefit all you meet.

My tongue is like the pen of a ready scribe. (Psalm 45:1)

Spirit of Wisdom, guide my daily efforts to communicate well.

Fits Her to a Tea

E-mails and telephone calls can be great ways to keep in touch. Yet, there's still something special about getting a card or note in the mail.

Carol Van Sickle of Washington, Pennsylvania, enjoys sending greeting cards to family and friends. And she doesn't stop there. She includes a teabag or two in each envelope. No wonder people call her "The Tea Lady."

Writing in *Guideposts*, Van Sickle says that she loves "the comforting customs associated with tea." So she sends Earl Grey or Darjeeling or mint or whatever she thinks her recipient would enjoy. She treasures "the thought of a friend taking a little quiet time away from her busy day to relax with a hot cuppa."

One friend told her that "even when we're far apart, teatime always brings us closer together."

Look for ways in your life to stay close to your loved ones.

The compassion of human beings is for their neighbors, but the compassion of the Lord is for every living thing. (Sirach 18:13)

My family and friends need my compassion. Jesus, open my eyes to the many chances You give me to touch them.

Ways to Say, "I Love You"

Let your dearest loved one know you care. Here are ideas from *Woman's Day:*

- Renee – "Gustavo deposits little love notes in my pockets, purse or suitcase."

- Karen – "Marc just started a high-pressure job, so I do little things to give him the extra TLC – playful text messages that will make him smile...a huge hug and kiss when he comes home."

- Rachel – "Simon dedicated an entire day to me... coffee and pastries in bed...flowers delivered to my office...dinner waiting when I came home. I felt truly special."

- Diana – "I often write little love notes in lipstick on the bathroom mirror."

Our loved ones thrive on our loving words, and our caring and thoughtful actions. Let them know they are loved, today.

> **Love is patient...kind...not envious or boastful or arrogant or rude. It does not insist on its own way; it is not irritable or resentful. ...(Love) rejoices in the truth. (1 Corinthians 13:4-6)**

Foster and bless loving relationships, Loving Father.

Imagine a Better Future

Homeless youngsters live a difficult day-to-day life, in shelters, motels, cars, even on the streets. For those who miss school, their future will be just as tough. Helping ensure these children realize a better tomorrow is up to adults.

"These kids didn't choose to be homeless, and they're going nowhere if they can't read or write," says Agnes Stevens, who founded School on Wheels (SOW) in Los Angeles.

Robert Rhone first met Stevens when he was 13 and living in a shelter. Today the insurance claims rep has fond memories of his tutor. "She always had time for us."

SOW has hundreds of volunteers who go out and find unschooled homeless kids. Then they provide tutoring as well as books and backpacks. They encourage parents and emphasize the importance of an education to their child's future.

Each of us can do something to help a homeless person today, if we only think about it and make the effort.

Jesus...was indignant and said..."Let the little children come to Me; do not stop them." (Mark 10:14)

Crucified Lord, give us the will to remedy homelessness.

Stones of Solace

Millie Sims of Champaign, Illinois, was grief-stricken when Arthur, her husband of 53 years, died suddenly. She found solace in the garden he had tended so lovingly.

One day, she noticed the small smooth river rocks he had gathered and arranged around the shrubs. Sims found comfort in just holding them. Then she marked four of them with the words faith, hope, love and peace, and put them in a bag, tied it with ribbon and gave them to a friend who was also bereaved. At Christmas, she did the same thing for dozens of shut-ins to whom her church was sending gifts.

Now, Sims has sent these "peace rocks" to people in 60 countries for birthdays, anniversaries and other occasions. She says that "by sharing them, I continue to be comforted."

If you are able to turn your pain and grief into service to others, you will gain more than you ever imagined.

The Father of mercies...consoles us in all our afflictions, so that we may be able to console those who are in any affliction.
(2 Corinthians 1:3,4)

Beloved Father, comfort us in our sorrow so that we may console others in theirs.

Time to Do More

When we're so busy with work, home and outside activities, it's hard to find time to stop and really think about our lives: where we are, where we're headed, where we are going.

John Rhoads offered these thoughts:

"Do more than exist, live.

Do more than touch, feel.

Do more than look, observe.

Do more than read, absorb.

Do more than hear, listen.

Do more than think, ponder.

Do more than talk, say something."

Let's try to pay more attention to ourselves and to the peace and joy God wants us to know and to share. Let's do more than survive. Let's choose to live.

Truly I tell you, whoever does not receive the kingdom of God as a little child will never enter it. (Mark 10:15)

My Savior, fill me with a zest for the life You want me to live for my own sake and that of those around me.

You Really Are What You Eat

When Sister Mary Tacheny, SSND, serves a meal, her guests know that what they see is what they get. That's because Sister Tacheny takes the purity of her food very seriously. When she says, "I believe we are what we eat," she is talking about more than basic nutrition.

She is one of a growing number of Americans who are becoming more mindful and careful about food. For example, Sister Tacheny is as concerned about the chemicals she's avoiding as about the nutritional content of what she serves.

Lutheran theologian L. Shannon Jung says that Westerners' disconnect from foods' origins disconnects them from God. In choosing processed fast food eaten on the run instead of more naturally grown, well-cooked food shared with loved ones around the table, "we have lost sight of God's greatest blessings, the earth and other humans."

Choose the food you eat wisely.

When the hour came, (Jesus) took His place at the table, and...He said to them, "I have eagerly desired to eat this Passover with you before I suffer. (Luke 22:14-15)

Jesus, remind us that the blessings of the communion table are reflected in meals shared with loved ones.

The Song of the Whale

Douglas Chadwick eased over the boat's gunwale and into the Pacific Ocean.

There, in front of him, suspended head down, pectoral fins spread was the humpback whale that had been singing. The whale, seven times his length and 400 times his weight, approached very closely, eyed him, passed over him at least three times. Meanwhile, Chadwick could hear and feel the songs of this whale and other humpbacks in the area.

Writing about his adventure in *Sierra* magazine, he says that he "felt wary and off balance but never really frightened. I was too overwhelmed." Chadwick "trusted that the force hovering before (him) was benign." The whale "showed no intention of doing anything except making inquiries after its fashion as an intelligent, purposeful, immanent being. It had questions."

All God's creatures are awe inspiring. All have as much right to life as we humans do. Respect them.

Will (Leviathan) speak soft words to you? (Job 41:3)

Creator, remind us that the creatures You formed exist to live the lives You planned for them—and to thrive.

Women Helping Women

Maria Otero began the non-profit Women's Venture Fund to offer advice, training, and money for women wishing to start their own businesses.

After 12 years of practicing law, Otero saw that women from underprivileged neighborhoods needed help. She decided to do something but, as she says, "My goal was never to become a micro-lender per se, but to create a place where women could access information, resources, and a community to support them in succeeding as entrepreneurs."

Otero's organization has helped over 12,000 New York City women willing to take a risk for something better with loans ranging from $200 to $15,000.

Never settle for less than you deserve. If you know you can work better, do better, or live better—plan carefully, then go for it.

He went on through cities and villages, proclaiming and bringing the good news of the kingdom of God. The twelve were with Him as well as some women...who provided for them out of their resources. (Luke 8:1-3)

Show us how to help those in need work better, do better or live better, Jesus.

Ensuring Care

While vacationing in Tahoe City, California, an idea for helping poor people came to Dr. Robert Forester as he stared at a pine tree, praying.

Not until he met another doctor, R.J. Heck, did the plan to make the idea a reality come together. Dr. Heck had survived a stroke in his 30s, and had been searching for a way to thank God, "to give something back."

The two formed a medical practice in which benefactor patients would pay a yearly sum for personalized boutique care, allowing the duo to provide medical care to other patients who are uninsured.

"We get to spend our entire day practicing medicine, and we get to do that in concert with our faith," says Dr. Forester.

What are your special gifts from God? How will you use them to bring God's love to others?

Like good stewards of the manifold grace of God, serve one another with whatever gift each of you has received. (1 Peter 4:10)

Abba, help me be a good steward of Your gifts.

Choosing to Be Human

We make so many choices everyday, some major, most quite minor. But do you ever think about the importance of decision-making for us as individuals? About how it's part of what makes us human?

"Everyone now alive has been charged with a sacred trust," said British historian Arnold Toynbee. "The making of choices is a heavy burden for us human beings; at the same time, our power to choose and to decide is an open door for hope. This God-given power is our distinctive human characteristic...

"At the price of being responsible, human beings are free. We are free to choose life and good or death and evil."

We should make every effort to base decisions, large and small, on thoughtful reasoning about what is right for us and our neighbors; what in our best judgment, accords with God's will.

If you choose, you can keep the commandments, and to act faithfully is a matter of your own choice. (Sirach 15:15)

Divine Master, guide me and all Your children in choosing wisely and well all that is for our welfare according to Your law of love.

Success in Four (Not-So-Easy) Steps

Corporate consultant John Miller believes that four simple questions can change your life. Miller offers these questions as a way to do some self-searching and to reach your highest potential:

- How can I be a good leader? Miller believes personal responsibility begins with the word "me."

- What can I do to make a difference? Miller reminds us of Mother Teresa, who said, "Do small things with great love."

- How can I help others achieve their goals? Encourage and motivate others with positive reinforcement whenever possible.

- How can I do my best? None of us are finished products. Seek progress, never perfection, in yourself and others.

Miller's approach to happiness and success is based on solid principles of personal responsibility and serving others. Try asking those four questions of yourself.

Live for the rest of your earthly life no longer by human desires but by the will of God. (1 Peter 4:2)

Direct us, Holy Spirit, toward the realization of our special purpose in life.

Red-Blooded Donors

If you or loved ones have ever needed a blood donation, you already appreciate all donors.

Many folks sign up for an annual blood drive, while some become regulars, donating every couple of months. That's as often as they are allowed, since the body needs that time to produce new red blood cells.

Then there's Wilbur Armstrong who lives in Hempstead, New York, and donates platelets every two weeks. Not only do the blood platelets have a relatively long shelf life, but they replenish themselves within days. Armstrong, a legally blind, retired electrical engineer, has been doing this since 1993.

One of the volunteer workers at the blood center says, "He feels he has to give back to the world. Imagine. I think he gives back quite a bit. He's very special."

Our world has so many needs and so many opportunities. Do what you can to contribute to "give back."

The whole law is summed up in a single commandment, "You shall love your neighbor as yourself." (Galatians 5:14)

Father, show me how to care for my neighbors the way I'd want them to care for me.

Oh Brother, What Great Puppets!

There's a fiddler on a roof, a piano player, a weight lifter and a trapeze artist, performing to the tune of "Stars and Stripes Forever."

Each is a puppet–a creation of Jesuit Brother Ed Sheehy. They reflect, he says, that "God is in all things."

The septuagenarian, who is a teacher and a coach, began his puppet ministry after being inspired by a sophisticated puppet exhibition on a trip to California.

Delighting audiences in public and Catholic schools, nursing homes, hospitals and churches for 30-plus years, Brother Ed has the same goal with each performance.

"You hope (it) brings some joy," he says. "Sometimes just putting a smile on someone's face can be the message."

The reason for a smile can come from the most unlikely source. Look around you carefully today–and smile!

The wise smile quietly. (Sirach 21:20)

In You, Beloved Christ, I find reasons to smile, reasons to hope. Thanks!

Sleep Tight, Little Ones

At age nine, Kassandra-Lynn Gonsalves read a story about foster children who lost their belongings while carrying them from home-to-home in plastic garbage bags. The thought of children losing what little they had inspired her to help.

With the help of her friends and family, Kassandra-Lynn created Good Night, Sleep Tight pillowcases.

The Fairhaven, Massachusetts, student assembles and decorates pillowcases filled with keepsakes including journals, address books, pens and stuffed animals. These items help foster children keep in touch with friends and families. Starting with only 100 pillowcases, she has since donated more than 1,000.

When asked about her gift-filled pillowcase, one young girl said "This makes me feel like I can start a new beginning."

We can help create "a new beginning" by sharing our kindness and generosity with others.

Show kindness and mercy...do not oppress the widow, the orphan, the alien, or the poor; and do not devise evil in your hearts against one another. (Zechariah 7:9,10)

Gentle Jesus, how can I help Your orphaned and abused children with my gifts of thoughtfulness, time and talents?

A Lifetime of Sisters

Throughout life many things change. Your heart will break; careers begin and end; children grow up; and distance will cause separations. But for women there's usually a constant—sisters. This may include your friends, mother, grandmother, and other female loved ones, as well as, of course, sisters.

A sister can guide you through bad times and help you celebrate the good times; offer a shoulder to cry on; walk down the aisle as a bridesmaid.

Some sisters are connected to us through blood. Others are from our neighborhoods, schools, work or church. Some we've known for years, others we haven't even met yet.

Women need other women. Who are your sisters? Do they know what meaningful role they play in your life?

The prophet Miriam, Aaron's sister, took a tambourine in her hand; and all the women went out...with tambourines and with dancing. And Miriam sang to them: "Sing to the Lord, for He has triumphed gloriously." (Exodus 15:20-21)

God, help women find meaningful ways to worship You in Spirit and in truth.

Hold On—For Dear Life

A small kitten survived a 70-mile trek on the New Jersey Turnpike by hanging tightly from the wheel well of an SUV.

No one knows how the then 8-month-old kitten, now named Miracle, became trapped there, but he held tight and survived despite singed fur and burnt paws. Discovered when another driver flagged down the driver of the SUV, the kitten was treated at a local animal shelter and put up for adoption.

It may seem a silly comparison—but if you think about it life can put us, too, in extreme situations. Yet no matter how bad things may seem in the moment, if you stay firm and persevere—if you hold on for dear life—the end can be better than you dared hope.

Life is worth all the effort you put into it.

Happy are those who persevere. (Daniel 12:12)

Holy Wisdom, encourage me to "hang in there," to persevere in growing into the person I was created to be.

Trust Your Instincts

Gail Blanke believes that it was because she listened to her "little inner voice" that she avoided potentially serious consequences when she started to feel ill.

Blanke refused to ignore what her instincts were telling her; even though her doctors said she was fine and that's what she wanted to believe. "I'm physically fit (I work out almost every day); I eat healthfully; I'm high-energy, optimistic."

A motivational speaker and author, Blanke was always the picture of health. Her electro-cardiograms were perfect and her blood pressure was normal.

Yet, Blanke developed a "bad feeling," a pressured, achy feeling in her chest. Although it only lasted about a minute before going away, it was significant. She turned out to be a candidate for bypass surgery, which was successful.

Now she advises other people to follow their instincts. If something doesn't feel right, ask questions.

Listen carefully. (Job 13:17)

Remind us, Caring Creator, that You give us wisdom. Help us to recognize and use it well.

The Light of Wisdom

Most people think of light bulbs when they hear the name Thomas Edison, and with good reason. Before he celebrated his thirtieth birthday, Edison had devised a multitude of electrical inventions, including the electric stock ticker and improved versions of existing telegraph equipment.

What many may not know is that Edison's career as an inventor was a lucrative one. By 1876, he had earned over $40,000 from his inventions–a staggering sum at the time.

Because Edison loved his work, he spent his money on scientific gadgets and research, living a simple, frugal life in order to continually reinvest in his pursuits. In fact, he risked nearly all of his savings to launch the world's first industrial research laboratory.

Sometimes, the very best cheerleader for your efforts is you. Reinforce your pursuits with positive encouragement from within. If you believe in yourself, others will follow.

Riches and strength build up confidence. (Sirach 40:26)

Transform me into a positive, upbeat, self-confident person, Blessed Trinity.

Helping Ugandan Children

Educator Mary Kafuko saw the horrible living conditions of the street children in Jinja, Uganda, and decided to become a social worker. That brought her into contact with "town girls," young girls who supported themselves and their children through prostitution.

Kafuko began the Adolescent Development Network (ADSN) so they'd have other ways to earn a living. At an ADSN trade school, for example, the young women learn to make clothing. Since many of the girls come to the city from nearby impoverished villages, Kafuko now works with some of the villages building schools, daycare centers, gardens and more.

Mary Kafuko saw a problem and didn't stop working until she had found a solution.

If you see something wrong and realize a change is needed, make that change. If you feel strongly about doing something, go do it. There's no time like the present.

Support the weak, remembering the words of the Lord Jesus, for He Himself said: 'It is more blessed to give than to receive'. (Acts 20:35)

Merciful Jesus, how can we end the various forms of degradation, exploitation and abuse against girls and women around the world?

When "Different" Isn't in the Dictionary

When Evan Ducker was born, his parents, Donna and Greg, were so happy that they did not care about the rose-colored "port wine stain" birthmark on his face.

Although birthmarks such as Evan's occur on one in every 100 babies in America, the Duckers started to hear the question, "What's wrong with his face?"

It was not until Evan, then age four, asked his mother why no characters in his books had a birthmark that Donna Ducker really paid attention to the mark.

"I'm sure there are plenty of books about birthmarks!" exclaimed his mother. But their search found none. So mother and son decided to write their own book; one in which individual differences are celebrated.

Buddy Booby's Birthmark hit bookshelves in 2006. Evan is often called a spokesman for kids like him.

Let's respect not only our similarities but our differences.

Jealousy and anger shorten life and anxiety brings on premature old age. (Sirach 30:24)

May we celebrate our differences each and every day, Creator of all.

Acts of Kindness

While Rosemary Colombraro was on vacation, she saw on the news that a cold front was moving towards her hometown. She was worried because of the new plants and citrus trees she had planted in her garden. But when Colombraro came home she saw the plants covered and the trees wrapped in blankets.

She found a note from a neighbor saying, "I've got you covered." Colombraro was deeply touched by the thoughtfulness.

Little acts of kindness mean a great deal. Here are a few ways to be a good neighbor: A simple hello to the new folks on the block or the new kid in school can brighten their day. Give old clothes that are still usable to a church or shelter. Volunteer your time at local charities.

It doesn't really take too much effort to help others. Yet it can mean all the difference in their day.

In everything do to others as you would have them do to you; for this is the law and the prophets. (Matthew 7:12)

Inspire our sharing, our caring, our loving compassion for each other, Abba.

A Real School of Rock

How did a Bronx, New York, elementary school go from so-so to one of the borough's top performers?

Rock 'n' roll—that's how! "When I first got here, the kids lacked confidence," said John Hughes, the principal of Public School 48. "They didn't think they deserved good teachers or good classrooms."

The principal-by-day is himself a rocker-by-night, playing guitar in a band called Johnny Seven. He used rock music to build self-esteem and spur academic achievement. Hughes started by treating the kids like rock stars—and playing rock music at the school. He compliments the young people—and praises the school itself.

"Now we've got a bunch of really confident kids here," explains Hughes.

Everybody's life has a special melody all its own. Open your ears and heart to find yours.

David took the lyre and played it...and Saul would be relieved and feel better, and the evil spirit would depart from him. (1 Samuel 16:23)

I sing Your praises, Divine Master, for You have sent me blessings in abundance.

Careers for Chocolate

What happens when two lawyers and a financial analyst spend time working with a master chocolatier? A sweet switch of jobs, that's what.

Kimberly Reindl, Peter Clement and Paul Allulis, friends from Baltimore, read about an Oregon-based company called Vocation-Vacations. Started by Brian Kurth—a former corporate executive who had seen his dad work for years in a job he hated—the firm offers people the chance to test-drive a dream by spending several days working with a pro in one of 75 job fields.

The Maryland trio signed up to work with Portland chocolate master Jack Elmer. Soon after, they quit their jobs and began ordering gear, testing recipes and preparing to open their new Baltimore chocolate store.

Change can be tough to make, but every once in a while it offers us the sweetest of solutions.

I will decide what to do. (Exodus 33:5)

You fill my life with good things, Faithful Lord, and for this, I praise You.

Teddy Bears Offer Comfort

Her grandmother's colon cancer diagnosis made a lasting impact on then seven year-old Taylor Crabtree.

After watching a news report about stuffed animals being given to traumatized kids, and knowing how her grandmother suffered, Taylor wanted to comfort kids in similar situations. She decided to provide teddy bears for children with cancer.

When word of her project spread, volunteers from local churches and Girl Scout troops got involved. Taylor, now a teen, has over 1,000 helpers, and has donated 20,000 teddy bears to kids across the country.

When asked about her mission, Taylor Crabtree said, "I'm just trying to ease their pain. When you have something to hold, it helps."

Each one of us can spread the message of God's love by comforting those who are in pain.

Comfort , O comfort My people, says your God. (Isaiah 40:1)

Remind us, Merciful Redeemer that the sick, the lonely and the depressed need hugs and embraces—the gentle human touch—to help them heal.

Forever Blowing Bubbles—in Glass

If you throw away an empty soda or beer bottle around Seikichi Inamine, chances are you'll see your trash again—as beautiful art glass.

Okinawa's premier glassmaker, Inamine is one of the few on the island who continues to use recycled glass as the base for his art pieces. The tradition started just after World War II when glassmakers resorted to melting old bottles—many of them discarded by U.S. service members—and reusing the material for common household glassware.

The bubbles produced in this process were seen as flaws by more commercial glass-blowers, and they abandoned the practice. But for this Japanese artisan, there is something "wondrous" in the air bubble flaws in the glass pieces he produces.

For all of us, the imperfections of our humanity are mixed with the spark of the divine.

I have filled him with divine spirit, with ability, intelligence, and knowledge...to devise artistic designs. (Exodus 31:3,4)

Master, guide my words and deeds by Your Spirit.

Passion Prayer

Rose and Gil had a good marriage and loved each other. But the pressures of life–children, jobs, finances and the like–took most of their energy and attention. What's a couple to do? On Marriage Encounter weekends, they found answers.

On the first weekend, Gil recalls, "through a lot of sharing of intimate thoughts and feelings, hopes and fears, our love began to overflow." Rose adds "our first step was…to share deeply and open our hearts completely to one another. This opened the doors to our passion!"

Later, a priest suggested that they "ask God to take away your inhibitions and to be totally filled with the love of your spouse. Pray for gentleness and selflessness." Rose says that they did "and received an amazing, spiritual experience."

Make time to cherish your spouse. And pray to God, whose passion created and sustains the world, to unleash the passion in your loving togetherness.

God is love, and those who abide in love abide in God and God abides in them. (1 John 4:16)

Triune God, strengthen and bless all loving relationships.

A Family Tree Grows in Brooklyn

Carmine Cincotta never planned to join his family's fruit and vegetable business. In fact, he pursued a corporate career after obtaining a history degree.

However, after losing interest in corporate work, Cincotta joined the family business that had been started in 1939 by his grandfather. He hasn't looked back since.

He and his father, Jimmy, work together in the Brooklyn storefront. It had been established in 1970, a time of lower rents, shifting demographics and long, hard workdays. Much has changed, except the long work days. But thanks to its history, the store remains a focal point for both new and old customers in the neighborhood.

Character and uniqueness can't be bought. They are qualities established over time, through hard work and care. Patronize independent businesses when possible. They help maintain a community's identity.

You shall have honest balances, honest weights: ...I am the Lord. (Leviticus 19:36)

Father, help us value and honor the traditions, uniqueness and independence of others.

Future Docs Help Out

"It's always been my dream to become a doctor...to help people and make them healthy," said medical student Omar Bennani. As chairman of Association H.O.P.E, Bennani and fellow medical students are working on a special project: helping people who lack adequate health care in Morocco.

While visiting villages, the students talk to people about disease prevention and taking care of themselves. Using their medical skills, the students offer villagers free healthcare and treatment.

"When I'm in the villages, I feel like I'm doing the work I should be doing everyday," said Bennani, who hopes to make participation in a program like this mandatory for medical students.

Using your skills is a wonderful way to give back to others. God made each of us special and gave everyone a special talent. Embrace that gift and use it to help those around you.

I have given skill to all the skillful.
(Exodus 31:6)

Holy Spirit, how can I help those less fortunate than myself with my gifts and talents?

Lead On

What makes a good leader?

The Economist magazine offers these ten key traits:

1. Act ethically. Set high standards for yourself.
2. Make difficult decisions. Face up to the facts.
3. See clearly. Focus clearly on problems.
4. Desire to create. Consider your legacy.
5. Communicate effectively. Speak clearly and truthfully.
6. Judge people accurately. Recognize strengths, weaknesses.
7. Develop talent. Mentor tomorrow's leaders.
8. Show maturity. Stand above petty jealousies.
9. Adapt quickly. Be willing to alter plans and opinions.
10. Win people over. Take time to develop loyalty.

If you want to lead, you have to serve. It's that simple and that hard.

The Son of Man came not to be served but to serve. (Mark 10:45)

Gracious God, thank You for the trust You've placed in me. Show me how to do my best.

When You Make a Mistake

Are you willing to admit your mistakes?

A story from the book *The Personal Touch* by Terrie Williams and Joe Cooney tells about a man who did just that.

After mailing some documents to a client, a businessman discovered a few typos. The client had been with his firm for a long time and was known as a stickler for detail. Though the businessman was tempted to ignore the situation, he realized that wasn't a solution. So, he corrected the copy and sent it to his client with an apology.

The client called to thank him, saying, "Most people wouldn't have bothered to do what you did. That shows me confidence and character. It's always refreshing to know that there are still people out there willing to own up to their mistakes."

Don't be afraid to say you've erred. It might sound trite, but it's still true: Nobody's perfect.

The truth will make you free. (John 8:32)

Paraclete, don't let me give in to fear. Help me to be truthful, especially when it's difficult.

"Subway Superman"

He's not faster than a speeding bullet, nor is he stronger than any locomotive, but Wesley Autrey is truly a hero.

While waiting for a New York City subway, a fellow passenger suffered a seizure and fell on the tracks as the train sped into the station. Autrey jumped down onto the tracks, but quickly realized he didn't have time to pull the man out.

Onlookers assumed the worst when the subway plowed over the two of them, but received the shock of their lives when the two emerged unscathed. Autrey had pinned the two of them to the trough below the tracks and escaped the screeching train by inches.

Though Autrey has become the toast of the town, he remains humble and selfless. "You should do the right thing," Autrey said. "I did it out of kindness. Not for recognition or glory."

Make a difference by doing the right thing out of kindness, today.

A Samaritan while traveling came near him; and...was moved with pity. He...bandaged his wounds...put him on his own animal, brought him to an inn, and took care of him. (Luke 10:33-34)

Give me courage to help those in need, God.

A Gift from the Past to the Present

Many cities celebrate St. Patrick's Day with parades, but the people of Syracuse, New York, have added a generous twist of their own.

Those attending the parade bring canned goods or bags of rice or dried beans which are collected as part of the St. Patrick Hunger Project. "Many groups collect food on Thanksgiving, but by March the food banks are usually low," says Bill Gooley who coordinates the event.

Thousands of pounds of food have reached local agencies assisting poor and hungry people. Gooley also reminds donors of their own history: "Many people came from Ireland because of the Great Famine. There was a parallel here."

Our backgrounds can provide us with wonderful traditions as well as a sense of our place in today's world. More than that, our history can connect us with our neighbors–who are not very different from us, after all.

Do not neglect to do good and to share what you have, for such sacrifices are pleasing to God. (Hebrews 13:16)

Divine Master, I thank You for my faith, my family, my heritage. Thank You, too, for the many blessings You give all Your children on Your good earth.

At Home in Church

As a youngster, Joel Pulis watched a relative struggle with bipolar disorder. It gave him a special sensitivity to the needs of those with mental illness.

As an adult doing outreach work for a church in Dallas, Texas, he realized that those with depression, schizophrenia and other problems rarely felt at home in traditional houses of worship. That's when Rev. Pulis founded the non-denominational Well Community for anyone with mental health problems.

In addition to weekly services, Pulis offers Bible classes, counsels church members, takes them to medical appointments and even helps them find homes. One parishioner says, "Here I don't have to go through the loneliness. It helps to reduce the stigma, takes the edge off. At least for a couple of hours a week we can be with our adoptive family. This is what church should be."

Every church can make an effort to welcome all God's children with acceptance and joy.

My house shall be called a house of prayer for all peoples. (Isaiah 56:8)

Remove the prejudice from my heart that blinds me to the needs of all of my brothers and sisters, Jesus, model of acceptance.

Planting Peace, Two Students at a Time

One of the most frustrating world conflicts is Northern Ireland's "Troubles" between Protestants and Catholics. Seamus Hodgkinson wanted to change that.

Hodgkinson, a teacher at Doane Stuart Middle School in Albany, New York, was raised in Northern Ireland during the bloody 1960s. The British Government's "solution" then was a barbed-wire topped 30-foot high brick wall between Catholic and Protestant neighborhoods.

Hodgkinson wondered if he could tear down that wall by bringing even one Catholic and one Protestant student together in the United States to learn new ideas and break through the hatred. After a decade of obstacles, his dream was realized. And by 2005 the Doane Stuart's Irish Exchange Program had won the Leading Edge Award for Equity and Justice from the National Association of Independent Schools.

God made each person in His image and likeness. How can we work together to promote peace and tolerance?

All who hate a brother or sister are murderers, and...murderers do not have eternal life abiding in them. (1 John 3:15)

Holy Spirit, counsel me so I can see myself and everyone else as our Father's beloved children.

A Humble Opinion

"People with humility don't think less of themselves. They just think about themselves less," say Ken Blanchard and Margret McBride in *The One Minute Apology*.

Humility has an image problem. It's fine to avoid being proud or vain, but who wants to be a doormat? And that's exactly how many of us view humility: as being unwilling or unable to stand up for ourselves.

Here's what writer Rabino Nilton Bonder says, "Many people believe that humility is the opposite of pride, when, in fact, it is a point of equilibrium. The opposite of pride is actually a lack of self-esteem. A humble person is totally different from a person who cannot recognize and appreciate himself as part of this world's marvels."

The essence of humility is truth. Rather than making too much or too little of yourself, look at yourself and your relationships with others and with God as honestly as you can.

The Pharisee, standing by himself was praying thus, 'God, I thank you that I am not like other people'...But the tax collector...was beating his breast and saying, 'God, be merciful to me, a sinner!' (Luke 18:11,13)

Merciful Savior, help me grow in true humility, true love of self, of neighbor, of You.

Divine Dentistry

Most of us are familiar with the work of traditional missionaries. But have you ever heard of dental missionaries?

Dr. Frank Serio and a team of other dentists are just that to an impoverished community in the Dominican Republic.

Each year for the past two decades, Dr. Serio joins his fellow dental missionaries in El Cercado, where they treat six or seven patients at a time in a makeshift dental office. Assisted by both practicing dentists and dental students, they provide much-needed dental care.

Dr. Serio's philosophy and approach are simple. He asks, "Did you leave the place better than you found it?" when evaluating the team's work each year.

Simple as that may be, it's not a bad way to approach life in general. Ask yourself each time you interact with others: Have I made a positive impact on this situation or person? Have I effected change for the better?

Do good and evil will not overtake you. Prayer with fasting is good, but better than both is almsgiving with righteousness. (Tobit 12:7-8)

Spirit of love, guide each of us in bringing positive change to the world, one deed at a time.

Patience, Patience

Kids are notoriously impatient creatures. Come to think of it, the same can easily be said for many adults.

Why is patience so hard for so many of us, especially in prayer? All of us at one time or another wonder, "Why hasn't God answered my prayers?" We may cry out as Jesus did from the cross, "My God, my God, why have You forsaken me?" (Matthew 27:46)

It may be that God has better things in store for us. Or, just as a parent doesn't always grant a child's wish for the child's good, so it may be with God. Perhaps, as the prophet Isaiah reminds us, "My thoughts are not your thoughts, nor are your ways My ways, says the Lord." (Isaiah 55:8)

What ever the reason–for who can know God's mind?–feel free to pour out your very impatience itself with God.

Why, O Lord, do You stand far off? Why do You hide Yourself in times of trouble? (Psalm 10:1)

Creator, help me trust that You have plans for my welfare and not for my harm; plans to give me a hope-filled future.

Coffee and Toast with a Side of Prayer

Breakfast can be more than ham and eggs.

Michael Gutwillig, writing in *Guideposts* magazine, tells about the Friday morning get-togethers he and other business people have at a restaurant in Montreal, Canada. They chat and then they pray. "The words come out in a mix of languages, English, Hebrew, Arabic, French—reflecting our different backgrounds," he says. "But we're together on one thing: praying and working for a better world."

The group has met for over 30 years, and while some have moved away or died, the informal breakfast and prayer club continues with new members. The regulars pay for the breakfast of each first-timer.

They pray about people and problems in the news; they pray for prisoners and others in trouble. Gutwillig adds, "Their faiths are as different as their faces and ages, but I've seen the same strong belief that our prayers make a difference."

Prayers—and concerned people—do indeed make a difference.

"Will not God grant justice to His chosen ones who cry to Him day and night? Will He delay long in helping them? I tell you, He will quickly grant justice to them." (Luke 18:7-8)

Enliven and enrich our prayers, God of all.

When Faith Is Hard

Have you ever had your faith tested?

Sir Thomas More, Lord Chancellor of England, refused to ask the pope to annul Henry VIII's marriage, nor would he recognize Henry as head of the church in England. By 1533, he was imprisoned, charged with high treason. Before being beheaded two years later, More wrote to his daughter Margaret about reliance on God:

"I will not mistrust Him, Meg, though I shall feel myself weakening and on the verge of being overcome with fear. I shall remember how St. Peter, at a blast of wind, began to sink because of his lack of faith, and I shall do as he did: call upon Christ and pray to Him for help. And then I trust He shall place His holy hand on me and in the stormy seas hold me up from drowning."

Fear can drive us to the brink of faith and hope. But God's love will yet find us.

Save me, O Lord, from my enemies; I have fled to You for refuge. (Psalm 143:9)

Spirit of Fortitude, hold me when I would turn away from You.

What is Prayer?

Some spiritual writers tell us not to force our feelings. Others recommend one method or another. Many speak of prayer as divorced from ordinary life.

But a column by Sister Margie Lavonis, CSC in the San Antonio, Texas, *Today's Catholic* newspaper, reminds us that we need to integrate prayer into our everyday life; to make conversation with God the very center of our lives.

To do that we first must know our own definition of prayer: Memorized prayers? The Rosary? Reading the Bible? Meditation? Liturgy?

Then Sister Lavonis suggests that we "set a realistic amount of time for prayer each day and use it to share with God the ordinariness of our lives, including our thoughts and feelings. It is our time to be real with God." She adds that it's "okay to talk with God at other times," too.

Be real with God. Let God be real with you. Today! Now!

Pray without ceasing. (1 Thessalonians 5:17)

Abba, help me be real with You, now, right now.

Just Clowning Around

Facing serious illness is hard. Finding a reason to smile can seem next to impossible, especially for children.

So, it's special when someone can coax a smile from an ailing youngster. But that's what Kim Winslow (aka Dr. Van Loon) does. This "doctor of delight," with the Big Apple Circus's Clown Care Unit, revels in the free rein he has to use his creativity to bring joy to hospitalized children. Some children are groggy from treatments; other youngsters want to get into the act. Winslow tailors his act accordingly.

"Being a clown is the only thing I've ever done. It's my life, my job, my income and it's taken me around the world," says Winslow.

The non-profit Clown Care now sends close to 100 clown "doctors" to 17 pediatric hospitals around the United States.

How can you bring joy to an ailing child?

(Jesus) went in where the child was. He took her by the hand and said to her, "Talitha cum," which means, "Little girl, get up!" (Mark 5:40-41)

Divine Physician, comfort sick children and their parents and families. Bring them Your healing.

Universal Design

Architect and designer, Michael Graves is known for "making good design accessible to the masses," at Target stores, for example.

Now, notes Louise Stone in the *AARP Bulletin*, Graves is bringing his skill and passion for good design to the medical-equipment field. When an infection left him paralyzed a few years ago, Graves was painfully introduced to a "grim new world where he was often at the mercy of poorly designed medical products."

Graves didn't like what he saw and set to work helping the home health-care industry improve the design of canes, flexible shower heads and the "reachers" that allow people in wheelchairs to grasp objects.

According to Stone, the redesigned products have "that Michael Graves style—rounded edges, soft handles, a touch of color and, often, of whimsy." Although meant primarily to accommodate the needs of people with disabilities, Graves' universal designs help everyone.

How can you use your experience to help others?

**Clothe yourselves with compassion.
(Colossians 3:12)**

Awaken my empathy, sympathy and compassion, Merciful Savior.

Freeing Forgiveness

In 1993, while working to register black voters for South Africa's first free election, 26-year-old Amy Biehl was killed by a mob intent on overthrowing the apartheid government.

Soon after, her parents, Linda and Peter Biehl, quit their jobs and moved from California to South Africa. They began a foundation in their daughter's name. Today, two of Biehl's killers work for that foundation.

"Forgiving is looking at ourselves and saying, 'I don't want to go through life feeling hateful and revengeful, because that's not going to do me any good,'" explains Linda.

If you decide to forgive someone, start first by acknowledging that you've been hurt. Putting that hurt in perspective, and then letting go of the weight and stress of your anger comes next.

In the final analysis, forgiveness of others and ourselves helps us face each new day choosing to live in peace.

Our Father in heaven...forgive us our debts, as we also have forgiven our debtors. (Matthew 6:9,12)

Heal our physical, mental and spiritual wounds, Caring Father. Help those whose debts are yet unforgiven.

Spreading Happiness

Deepak Chopra's most influential mentors were his father, a well-known cardiologist, and his mother, a homemaker.

Once a week, his father treated patients free of charge. People from across India consulted him. He explained their conditions to them, wrote prescriptions and paid for the medicine himself. Chopra's mother cooked food for them and paid for their bus or train fare. Chopra and his brother would escort the patients in to see their father.

When all the patients had left, Chopra's parents talked to the children about the day. "And the moral of the lesson always was that if you want to be happy, then you have to make somebody else happy," writes Chopra.

As the song says, "Happiness runs in a circular motion." People gain happiness from making others happy. When these people help others they go on to create a circle of happiness. Reach out to help someone today.

I will leave in the midst of you a people humble and lowly....They shall do not wrong and utter no lies. ...They will pasture and lie down, and no one shall make them afraid. (Zephaniah 3:12,13)

How can I make even one other person happy today, now, Jesus?

Cost of Living?

From day to day, we don't always notice how prices change on big ticket items as well as daily necessities and amenities. But *American Heritage* magazine looked back at the cost of living in the U. S. in 1964 and the prices are stunning by today's standards. Here are a few examples:

- A four-bedroom, two-bath house in South Bend, Indiana sold for $16,000; a "penthouse view" Manhattan apartment rented for $245 a month.
- A Hershey chocolate bar cost $.05.
- A McDonald's hamburger cost $.15.
- A movie ticket cost $1.
- First class postage was $.06.
- The cost of a Ford Mustang started at $2,368.
- A gallon of regular gasoline cost $.27.

Times do indeed change, and we sometimes forget how much. But the essence of our lives still rests not on how much we spend, but on how much we give of ourselves, our time, our passion. Live your life to its fullest.

We have gifts that differ according to the grace given to us. (Romans 12:6)

Holy Spirit, grant me the ability to use all my talents for my own true welfare and the welfare of others.

Girls Get Second Chance

Los Angeles' Homegirl Café combines Patricia Zarate's cooking talents with her desire to help young women. The Café gives young women, former gang members and lawbreakers, training in cooking and preparing food as well as in responsibility and dedication.

While some businesses won't hire anyone with a criminal record, Homegirl Café helps young women with this exact problem. Zarate believes in second chances and gives young women an opportunity for a better life. Since many of these young women are mothers, family members watch their youngsters, allowing them to continue working.

We all do some things we later regret. That's why there are second–and more–chances which let us get our lives back on track.

Taking chances on another person can result in the sweetest rewards.

But we had to celebrate and rejoice, because this brother of yours was dead and has come to life; he was lost and has been found. (Luke 15:32)

Moment by moment You give us another chance, Merciful Redeemer. Inspire us to extend this same kindness to others.

Jovenes para Cristo

Over the years, Florencia Aranda watched the Spanish choir for children at Chicago's St. Philomena Parish grow.

But Aranda worried because there was no youth ministry for these children as they matured.

That changed the year Jovenes para Cristo (Youth for Christ) got started in the heavily Latino parish. It helps adolescents set goals and grow spiritually. Teens raise funds for the parish, collect food for the food pantry, serve on church committees, teach religion and sing in the Spanish choir.

"They will come to realize that they are an important part of the Body of Christ and the community needs them, their talents, creativity and love."

Do all you can to help children and teens know that their church belongs to them as well as to adults; that they are welcomed with open arms and open hearts.

Baptized into Christ...there is no longer Jew or Greek...slave or free...male or female...you are one in Christ Jesus...Abraham's offspring, heirs according to the promise. (Galatians 3:27-28,29)

Thank You, Divine Father, for blessing us through the waters of baptism.

Love and Duty

"Establishing relationships is more important than taking in money," said restaurant owner Sameer Jbari.

These sentiments wouldn't be that unusual for a popular neighborhood hang out. However, the restaurant Habayibna, which means loved ones, and the owner are in the Sadr City neighborhood of Baghdad.

In May, 2005, a car bomb burned and devastated the restaurant, but rather than close Jbari sold his family's house for $100,000 and rebuilt.

While Jbari hasn't yet earned back his costs, that wasn't as important as the owner's feeling of responsibility. He has more than 300 customers. And he employs 150 men and "that means 150 families are depending on me."

Loyalty to one's employees and their families as well as to customers should be important in every business. Let's respect all who work for their daily bread—including ourselves.

From everyone to whom much has been given, much will be required. (Luke 12:48)

Remind managers and employees to value each other and to treat each other with profound respect, Carpenter from Nazareth.

A Holiday for Foolishness

Holidays are celebrated for all sorts of reasons, but April 1st is the only holiday that celebrates foolishness.

Although there's some uncertainty about how the tradition of April Fools' Day began, it's most likely that this celebration traces its way back to 16th century France. Up until that time, the accepted calendar was the Julian calendar, which observed the beginning of the New Year around April. In 1564, King Charles IX declared that France would begin using the Gregorian calendar, which changed New Year's Day to January 1st.

But not everyone accepted the shift. These unfortunate souls were mocked as "fools," with people inviting them to bogus parties and sending them silly gifts.

Today, April Fools' Day gives each of us the opportunity to laugh a bit—the best medicine, really, for any day of the year.

Rejoice and exult with all your heart. (Zephaniah 3:14)

In the laughter of this day, Lord, help me to experience the joy of Your love.

What Can You Do?

As a young man in Bangladesh, Yasmin Assar's grandfather became blind in one eye due to a botched surgery.

Recalling her grandfather's struggle, the young teen from Stone Mountain, Georgia, set out to help others with impaired vision. The teen set up drop boxes around her hometown to collect used eyeglasses. She also enlisted a local non-profit, the Georgia Lions Lighthouse Foundation, to assist her with shipping the glasses to developing countries.

Through her efforts, thousands of eyeglasses have been sent to Romania, Ghana, Bangladesh, and Honduras.

Inspired by her drive and determination, Christina Lennon, executive director of the Lighthouse Foundation, often tells Yasmin Assar's story and asks the question, "If she's 16 and can do this, then what can you do?"

Develop the vision to help others.

The blind man said to Him, "My teacher, let me see again. Jesus said to him, "Go; your faith has made you well." Immediately he regained his sight and followed Him on the way. (Mark 10:51-52)

There are so many kinds of blindness, Divine Physician. Grant Your help and healing.

Ways to Nourish Friendships

All of us want to maintain close friendships. But it's hard given the hectic pace of our lives. *Women's World* magazine suggests these five tips to help you stay connected:

1. Synchronize your lives. If you rarely get to visit, try to read the same books or watch the same programs so you'll have something in common to share when you finally get together.

2. Embrace Technology. Try e-mails, text messages or online photos. Consider creating an online journal.

3. Schedule play dates. Arrange to send your kids to the same ballet or karate classes so you can catch up during class.

4. Remember special dates. Send cards or notes (real or online) for birthdays or anniversaries.

5. Use little chunks of time. Use your cell phone for a quick hello while walking the dog or standing on line.

Nourish your friendships and your spirit.

Wine and music gladden the heart, but the love of friends is better than either. (Sirach 40:20)

Bless us with loyal friends, Jesus.

Getting the Measles, Finding Life's Goal

At 15, Ron Meyer was spending his days hanging out with other high school dropouts in his West Los Angeles neighborhood. Today, he's president and chief operating officer of Universal Studios.

The transition started while he was in the Marine Corps and quarantined with the measles. Meyer's mother sent him two books: one about a street gang and another about a man in a talent-agency. "I realized," he says, "that I was no longer that idiot kid, and I wanted to change my life."

Setting out to do just that, he took any job he could, from busboy to short order cook. While working at a clothing store, Meyer heard about a messenger job at a talent agency. He had a good boss and learned a lot. From there, the path led to Universal.

Creating change in life–big or small–begins with the decision to make it happen.

Do not turn aside from the decision.
(Deuteronomy 17:11)

As I travel life's highway, Almighty God, direct me to the path that will best serve You.

Not Your Usual Food Bank

From the looks of it, the Greater Pittsburgh Community Food Bank looks like a modest office building. But that belies the anything-but-modest efforts that go on inside to feed the hungry.

After 25 years of operation, the Food Bank has grown to distribute 1.5 million pounds of food and other necessary items to approximately 350 member agencies that serve more than 120,000 individuals.

The demographics of the Food Bank's clientele, according to Ivy Ero, the director of educational programs, are unusual: only one percent is homeless; more than 70 percent has at least a high school diploma. Many are employed, but, even working full time, they can not feed their families and pay for housing, healthcare, transportation and clothing, too.

The number of people this food bank serves hints at the quandary millions of working poor Americans live every day. Support efforts to alleviate this burden on our neighbors in need.

To one who works, wages are not reckoned as a gift but as something due. (Romans 4:4)

Carpenter of Nazareth, remind employers that a living wage is the right of workers.

Canvas of Courage and Hope

An art project launched in a small South African town is giving global citizens greater awareness of the African AIDS epidemic.

The Keiskamma Altarpiece, a tapestry of embroidery and beadwork measuring 22 feet wide and 13 feet tall, was displayed at the International AIDS conference in Toronto. Since then, it has moved to other sites in an effort to raise awareness of the scope of Africa's AIDS problem.

The altarpiece was begun in Hamburg, South Africa. One-third of the town's 3,000 residents are HIV-positive; 90 percent are unemployed. Yet the altarpiece contains New Testament scenes of hope and life, health and recovery—the goal for the beleaguered town and for Africa.

As one project coordinator says, "The people of Hamburg could have easily surrendered to what was happening to them. But the women in the community fought back."

While there's hope, there's opportunity..

Why do you see the speck in your neighbor's eye, but do not notice the log in your own eye? (Luke 6:41)

Divine Physician, help scientists find a cure for HIV/AIDS. And, meanwhile, help us prevent its spread.

Too Stressed Out?

Whether it's an argument with a spouse, getting stuck in traffic or a misunderstanding with a co-worker, at some point today, you'll probably experience stress.

Here are three tips to avoid blowing up:

- Take a deep breath and count to ten, or say a brief prayer.
- Ask yourself what's causing the stress and whether or not it's really serious.
- Get away from the situation; find someone with whom you can talk.

Writer Wayne Muller suggests, "Let us take a collective breath, rest, pray, mediate, walk, sing, eat and take time to share the unhurried company of those we love. Let us, for just one day, cease our desperate striving for more, and instead taste the blessings we have already been given, and give thanks. God does not want us to be exhausted: God wants us to be happy."

Realizing God wants us to be happy is a good place to start.

Six days you shall labor and do all your work. But the seventh day is a Sabbath to the Lord your God; you shall not do any work. (Deuteronomy 5:13-14)

Loving Savior, calm our minds and hearts, lift our burdens.

The Legacy of Sigmund Freud

Love him or hate him, there's no denying Sigmund Freud has been influential on our times.

Decades after his death, the Viennese father of psychoanalysis still has an impact that is felt in boardrooms and classrooms; in laboratories and libraries. Literature and film wouldn't be the same without his work, even though much of it has been widely debunked.

"He was wrong about so many things," says University of Michigan psychologist James Hansell for a *Newsweek* article marking Freud's 150th birthday. "But he was wrong in such interesting ways. He pioneered a whole new way of looking at things."

Each one of us can define how we will be remembered tomorrow by the way in which we lead our lives today. What legacy do you hope to leave?

The teaching of the wise is a fountain of life, so that one may avoid...death. (Proverbs 13:14)

Give us, Holy Spirit, wise, discrete and caring friends in whom we can confide.

"Facing Danger, with God's Strength"

Speaking on German radio in 1933, young Lutheran pastor and prominent theologian, Dietrich Bonhoeffer said, "A man who lets himself be worshipped mocks God." The rest of the program was cut off by the Nazis.

For two years, Bonhoeffer directed a clandestine seminary. When it was closed, he went to New York, but instead of staying, he returned to Germany to work for an end to Hitler's regime.

Bonhoeffer was arrested in 1943 and held in solitary confinement for 20 months. Time in concentration camps and a mock trial followed. "Prisoner Bonhoeffer," he was told after the trial, "you are guilty of high treason."

Then early on April 9, 1945 Pastor Dietrich Bonhoeffer was hung, naked, from a gallows in the Flossenburg prison yard.

He had written, "The will of God is not a system of rules...(but) must be found new each day as we walk in God's presence."

I said, "Here I am; in the scroll of the book it is written of me. I delight to do Your will, O my God; Your law is within my heart." (Psalm 40:7-8)

Crucified and Risen Jesus, give us Your courage and strength to follow You.

Women Drivers

Although Danica Patrick dazzled with her driving excellence at the 2006 Indy 500, she wasn't the first woman to make history behind the wheel.

Almost a century ago, in 1909, Alice Ramsey was hired to drive a new car model cross-country from New York to San Francisco. The 22-year-old was more than up to the challenge, completing the trip in 59 days, better time than any man who had made such a drive before her.

Ramsey's many driving success stories prompted other women to buy their own vehicles.

Then there's Janet Guthrie who, in the 1970s, cracked the male-dominated sport of oval-track auto-racing. As a lasting testament to her achievements, her helmet and driving suit are housed at the Smithsonian.

Sometimes, daring to do things a little differently can help drive things in a new—and better—direction.

Be strong and of good courage, and act. (1 Chronicles 28:20)

No matter what I do this day, Holy God, may Your Spirit be my guide and my inspiration.

Love-Work on It!

In India, researchers studied the differences between couples who married for romantic love and couples in arranged marriages.

Couples in romance-inspired marriages reported a decrease in their feelings of love after five years, but couples in arranged marriages felt more love over the years.

Perhaps it's because couples in arranged marriages knew from the start that loving actions and attitudes would be needed to inspire feelings of love in their partners. They never took love for granted. They knew work was involved.

So, married couples: Choose to respect and love each other each moment, each day, every day. Do fun things together. Resist the urge to quarrel in moments of anger or frustration. Listen to, respect and understand your partner's feelings. Support one another's emotional and personal growth. Express respect, love, appreciation and admiration for your spouse's qualities.

Never take love for granted. Choose to love.

Love is strong as death, passion fierce as the grave. ...Many waters cannot quench love, neither can floods drown it. (Song of Solomon 8:6,7)

Guest at Cana, bless couples with enduring yet ever fresh love.

Helping Patients Get Through Tough Time

People with cancer have a lot to struggle with: concerns about life, death, family and financial issues and more. Then there are the many side-effects of chemotherapy which usually include losing one's hair.

That's why several women at St. Michael and All Angels Episcopal Church in Studio City, California, started a Wig Exchange in 2001. Every year, they carefully clean and pass along hundreds of wigs that have been donated by individuals, Hollywood studios and the American Cancer Society.

Nancy Woods, who heads the project, says, "These women need to feel better. If they think they don't look well, they won't go out in public. But with a nice wig in a cute modern style, there's such joy."

God offers us so many ways to serve others. Look around you to see how you can help your neighbors in need. Something that seems so simple can mean so much.

Good works are conspicuous. (1 Timothy 5:25)

Loving Lord, we can ease the burdens and anguish of others in so many ways. Teach us to serve You in others.

Kindness Tapped Him on the Shoulder

Some time ago, Arthur Caliandro, senior minister of Manhattan's Marble Collegiate Church (Reformed), who's also a speaker and an author, went to Virginia's Shenandoah Valley to write.

At first, he was glad to be away from countless appointments and long meetings. But on Sunday morning, as he watched people at the town church greet one another and share bits of local news, he suddenly felt lonely. The feeling lasted throughout the service.

At the end, as he stood up to put on his overcoat, he felt a tap on his shoulder. An elderly lady said to him, "You're a visitor here. I'm very glad you came."

All these years later, Caliandro remembers those few simple words–that kindness which changed everything for him that morning.

William Wordsworth said that the best parts of a good person's life are "the little, nameless, unremembered acts of kindness and love."

Commit acts of kindness today.

The fruit of the Spirit is love, joy, peace, patience, kindness, generosity, faithfulness, gentleness and self-control. (Galatians 5:22)

Help me to show Your kindness and mercy to others this day, Holy Wisdom.

Before You Get Angry, Give Thanks

In 1912, the Clarks, a Scottish family, scrimped, saved and sacrificed for a long-awaited move to the United States. The 11 family members could hardly contain their excitement.

Then just one week before their ship was to sail, the youngest Clark boy was bitten by a dog. Because of the possibility of rabies, the entire family had to be quarantined for 14 days. The long-awaited trip was off. At first, they wept at their misfortune. They even got angry at God for what had happened.

But, a few days later, news of the sinking of the Titanic on its maiden voyage with the loss of over 1,500 women, children and men raced around the world. That was the very ship on which the Clarks were supposed to have sailed.

There are no easy answers to why some people survive tragedies and others don't. That's why we need to trust God always.

Another book was opened, the book of life. And the dead were judged according to their works. ...And the sea gave up the dead that were in it. (Revelation 20:12,13)

Adoni, both in life and in death we are Yours. Hear us as we "cry to Thee, for those in peril on the sea!"

Staying on the Job

One man went from full-time manager at Shell Oil to part-time project person there. After almost four decades with IBM, a woman is teaching math a few days a week at a local middle school.

Both are experiencing a new work stage: the not-quite-retirement. As life spans lengthen, pensions tighten and workplace rules change, going from full-time work to full-time leisure appears less realistic, less affordable and, to some, less desirable. That has led to the so-called bridge job which may be part-time.

"Why go from 100 m.p.h. to zero?" queries Joseph Quinn, a Boston College economist who co-authored a paper on the subject. "You wouldn't do that in your car. You'd do 70, then 50, then 20."

Companies who employ older employees also benefit from their experience and wisdom as well as their loyalty and productivity.

We all need to contribute and to have our work respected.

Rich experience is the crown of the aged. (Sirach 25:6)

Bless the work of older workers, Lord, and let them receive the respect they deserve.

Keeping Balance by Helping Others

When Lori Erickson first began volunteering at a local soup kitchen, she felt "a sense of virtuous self-satisfaction." She patted herself on the back for finding time in her busy schedule to help less fortunate people.

But, as time passed, she began to truly connect with the poverty and difficult life circumstances of many of the kitchen's clients. She says, "It was the first time I truly understood that volunteers receive more than they give."

Erickson has since taken on work as a hospice-care volunteer, a commitment that has enriched the blessings she receives through volunteering. "I often arrive feeling rushed and hurried, but as the minutes pass, I find a chance to breathe, reflect and think," she says.

Seen through this perspective, perhaps even the busiest among us could achieve more balance through volunteering to help others. Think about what you could give–and gain.

Be rich in good works. (1 Timothy 6:18)

Awaken in us a desire to give of our time, Spirit of Wisdom.

Freedom of Body and Soul

Matthew Sanford was 13 years old when a devastating car crash claimed the lives of his father and older sister—and left him paralyzed from the waist down.

Though he'd been athletic as a youngster, he concentrated on developing his mind, eventually earning a master's degree in philosophy. Then a friend suggested that he study yoga. Learning to focus on his arm strength and sense of balance, and, by using his hands to position his legs, Sanford mastered dozens of poses.

In 1997, he started teaching yoga to other physically challenged people at a rehabilitation center in Minneapolis. Five years later, he opened his own studio where he teaches those without handicaps, as well.

One student says of Sanford, "I see what he's done in his life and it inspires me to do more with my own life."

Whatever our abilities or disabilities, we can probably do far more that we think, if we give ourselves the chance.

We have become partners of Christ, if only we hold our first confidence firm to the end. (Hebrews 3:14)

Guide me in developing my gifts and talents according to Your plan, Blessed Trinity.

The Call of the Divine

If you read her business card, you'd know her as Maria Slizys, Real Estate Agent, but little about who she really is.

Her card won't tell you that Slizys' favorite saint is Joan of Arc, and that she loves taking nature walks. She's also an extrovert who enjoys her job. "I love the feeling of being able to assist someone in buying their first home," she says.

Nor will her card tell you that facing mid-life, Slizys became restless. She opted to take a program called Life Choices offered by the Adorers of the Blood of Christ, a group of religious sisters.

Many of the 1,500 people who have taken the program do it to discern religious vocations, but others use the various surveys, questionnaires and conversations to grow spiritually or seek the right job for them. Slizys is still contemplating her choices.

Titles tell us so little about God's wondrous human beings. Our depth, breadth and beauty can't be discerned in a glance.

Do not judge, so that you may not be judged. (Matthew 7:1)

Abba, help me see the danger of making snap judgments about others.

Return those Library Books—ASAP

Over 600 libraries in the United States have decided on a new way to make people return overdue library books and DVDs. Unique Management Services (UMS), a collection agency, calls at home and then informs credit bureaus if items are not returned. Working with UMS has resulted in 50-70 percent of people contacted returning library property.

Libraries are cracking down because they are losing money. Every book borrowed from the library and not returned, means one more book the library has to replace.

Taking a book that's not yours keeps it away from someone else. If you have something that doesn't belong to you: library books, DVD rentals, whatever, return them. Don't keep them from others or cost libraries and companies unnecessary expense.

Let's show honesty and honor in our own lives.

Then (Moses) took the book of the covenant, and read it in the hearing of the people; and they said, "All that the Lord has spoken we will do, and we will be obedient." (Exodus 24:7)

Remind us, Lord, to express our gratitude and integrity in all we do.

The Meaning of Everything

Here's a story that might be useful to remember if you're ever feeling a bit complaisant

An old rabbi told his students, "Everything in God's Creation is there for a purpose and a reason, therefore it has meaning."

One rather smug student asked, "In that case, what's the purpose of heresy, of denying the existence of God?"

'Ah, that heresy is indeed purposeful," answered the rabbi. "For when you are confronted by another who is in need, you should imagine that there is no God to help, but that you alone can meet this person's needs."

When life is going along well for us, it's all too easy to forget that we always and everywhere dwell in God's presence–and at His pleasure. How could we help others without God? How could we help ourselves? How?

Lord, You have searched me and known me. ...Even before a word is on my tongue, O Lord, You know it completely. You hem me in behind and before, and lay Your hand upon me. (Psalm 139:1,4-5)

Thank You, Creator and Lover of all things seen and unseen. Thank You, above all, for Yourself.

Youngsters Overcome Big Challenges

Change was hard for Mikael Jones. And now, he was on the verge of something really new and different.

"I expect him to have a little withdrawal. With everything new he has a problem at first," Lindy Jones said about her son. Mikael even found trying out a new pair of shoes daunting.

But Mikael has now graduated from the Children's Learning Center at the Helen Keller Services for the Blind. He's leaving the safety and comfort of his preschool for an unknown world with its new teachers, new rules, and new environment. All of this is a particular challenge for a blind youngster

Mikael and his classmates are learning a valuable lesson and, with hard work, love and support, they will meet the challenge.

Everyone has to find ways to cope with change, one of life's constants.

Then the eyes of the blind shall be opened, and the ears of the deaf unstopped; then the lame shall leap like a deer, and the tongue of the speechless sing for joy. (Isaiah 35:5-6)

Inspire us to face life's changes with courage and openness, caring Father.

Making Jobs Work

Tom Rath, a pollster with the Gallup Organization, specializes in studying attitudes toward work. His research reveals a workforce that's generally unhappy on the job. In fact, he says that dissatisfied employees cost between $250 and $300 billion in lost productivity each year in the United States.

The solutions according to Rath include giving praise and recognition, promoting positive interactions and relationships, and concentrating on each employee's strengths.

His research confirmed the positive management style his grandfather had taught him. "'Good job, Tom,' he would say," Rath recalls, thinking back to the snack stand he started at age 10, "and then my granddad would follow that up with something that told me he was really paying attention."

All we do, on the job or seeing that the job gets done, should give praise to the Creator who blesses us all.

I by my works will show you my faith. ...For just as the body without the spirit is dead, so faith without works is also dead.
(James 2:18,26)

May I always honor You, Lord of love, in my thoughts, words and deeds.

Giving to Those in Need

Thanks to Father James Ruggieri's And You Fed Me program at St. Patrick and St. Casimir parishes, homeless people in Providence, Rhode Island, receive not only food, but also clothing: socks, gloves, jackets, and more.

Volunteers gather clothing and distribute it every other week. They enjoy helping because they can tell how grateful the people are to receive such gifts. "We've started to develop relationships with these people," said one volunteer.

We all clean out our closets once in awhile. Instead of throwing those clothes away, find out where you can donate them. Many churches and other organizations accept clothing for the homeless. Others run thrift shops for low income neighbors.

Think of of ways you can clothe a needy person.

Come, you that are blessed by My Father, inherit the kingdom prepared for you from the foundation of the world; for I was...naked and you gave Me clothing. (Matthew 25:34-35,36)

Help us to see You, Sweetest Jesus, in our poorly clad neighbors. May their plight inspire us to donate clothing we no longer use.

Guilty Until Proven Innocent

The ideal is "innocent until proven guilty" and fortunately that's often the case. But, for some, the reality is different and they need help proving their innocence. Enter the Innocence Project, a nonprofit legal endeavor with a good track record of getting wrongfully accused prisoners released based on DNA evidence.

While it's heart-wrenching to hear stories of innocent people denied freedom for decades, for crimes they didn't commit, it's truly heart-warming when they're released due to their own determination and the expertise of the Innocence Project.

Alan Newton was one such man. He spent 22 years in New York's maximum-security prisons convicted of rape, robbery and assault. He was finally exonerated of these crimes which he had never committed.

Vindication is only the beginning. Ex-prisoners need continued support as they transition back to life as free members of society.

Let the groans of the prisoners come before You; according to Your great power preserve those doomed to die. (Psalm 79:11)

Free those unjustly convicted and imprisoned, Liberator.

Turning Surplus into Cash

If you think you've accumulated a lot of junk around your house, think how much more your state has lying around.

That's why a number of states hold auctions—in person or online—to sell used property that would once have been headed for the trash. Dick Graves, president of the National Association of State Agencies for Surplus Property, says "You need more money everywhere. There is wealth sitting here with some of this stuff."

"This stuff" ranges from a life-size Smokey the Bear statue to dump trucks and police cruisers to confiscated fishing gear and penknives. In addition to the money added to state coffers—as much as a $1.5 million annually—hundreds of tons of junk is kept out of landfills.

Some situations really can be win-win: we simply need to pay attention to problems and get creative.

Decide with equity for the meek. (Isaiah 11:4)

Open my mind to new and useful ways of approaching problems, Holy Spirit.

Putting Persistence in Its Place

What attributes make somebody successful? Ability? Intelligence? Upbringing? Sheer good fortune?

According to Calvin Coolidge, "Nothing in the world will take the place of persistence. Talent will not; nothing is more common than the unsuccessful person with talent.

"Genius will not; unrewarded genius is almost a proverb.

"Education will not; the world is full of educated derelicts.

"Persistence and determination alone are omnipotent. The slogan 'press on' has solved and always will solve the problems of the human race."

Certainly, people need a combination of factors to achieve their goals. But there is no doubt that little of value is ever accomplished without simple dogged determination. "Press on" is not a bad slogan for anyone who wants to succeed in doing good.

Be persistent. (2 Timothy 4:2)

Guide me, Blessed Trinity, in doing all that is right. Grant me the resolve to persist in my efforts so that I may accomplish good according to Your will.

God: Who is She, Really?

Simply asking that question undoubtedly raises eyebrows and more than a few tempers. After all, we're used to thinking of God as male.

Kathleen McVay, a scholar who studies ancient Aramaic depictions of God, has another viewpoint. Her research reveals that the Aramaic language, spoken daily by Jesus and His apostles, used a feminine pronoun for the Holy Spirit for Christianity's first four hundred years.

Immaculate Heart of Mary Sister Nancy Lee Smith, who is an iconographer, says, "The (Aramaic) language is based in poetry...as opposed to the philosophical Greek and the legal Latin."

Inspired by these findings, she did a series of paintings based on Aramaic hymns of St. Ephrem written in the fourth-century. "I wanted to do a visual, theological bridge for people," says Sister Smith who is trying to open up perspectives on the Divine.

Who is God for you?

I took them up in My arms...I led them with... kindness, with... love. I was...like those who lift infants to their cheeks. I bent down to them and fed them. (Hosea 11:3,4)

Remind me, God, that You called Yourself, "I Am Who I Am." Help us open ourselves to see You in the spirit of faith, hope and love.

Chickens Help the Environment

Among those living in the city of Diest, Belgium, 2,000 are receiving an unusual gift: three chickens each!

According to *Kippenmail,* a digital newsletter of "Adopteer een kip" ("Adopt a chicken"), a Dutch animal-rights organization, chickens can recycle biodegradable trash because they're omnivores that will eat kitchen leftovers.

The entire process is beneficial: one chicken can eat about nine pounds of kitchen garbage a month. In return, it lays eggs. And its dung can fertilize the garden. Multiply that by three chickens and that's 27 pounds of kitchen garbage disposed of inexpensively.

Until this program, recycling biodegradable garbage has been costly for Diest: half a million euros ($600,000 U.S.) a year.

Chickens may never replace the family dog, but their use in Belgium points in the right direction. There are simple solutions to many ecological problems if only we go to nature for help.

The Lord...formed the earth. ...He did not create it a chaos, He formed it to be inhabited! (Isaiah 45:18)

Inspire us to be careful conservators of the earth and the creatures You have formed, Creator.

One Small Step at a Time

Youth minister Lawrence Park, along with his youth group from Los Angeles, went to Rosarito, Mexico to help Columban Father Tony Mortell at his medical mission.

Neither Park nor Rev. Mortell expected the young people to be as dedicated as they proved they were. At first, while the line of patients grew longer, the youths seemed to be more interested in talking about *American Idol.*

Yet, despite their limited Spanish, Park saw the young people engage each patient with care and concern and quickly showed their eagerness to help in any way they could.

"Their eyes lit up with the realization that they could indeed help improve another person's quality of life, even if it is just one small step at a time," said Park.

Do you know a teen who could benefit from involvement with others today?

Train children in the right way. (Proverbs 22:6)

Through volunteer opportunities help us help teens to mature into caring, sharing adults, Jesus.

Watching the Church in Action

Emotional, fulfilling, sometimes draining it may be, but the work of volunteers at the Clare House of Hospitality in Bloomington, Illinois, is never boring.

"People who work here say this is the Church in action," says Tina Sipula, founder of the center, which feeds hundreds of people each day.

Clare House is more than just a soup kitchen, though. The homeless and needy see the center as a safe haven, says Sipula, where they find more than food. "It gives them a sense of dignity," she says. "They don't come for the soup as much as they come to be treated with respect and dignity."

Sipula cites her reliance on prayer for her ability to continue to be her brothers' and sisters' keeper.

Helping others is not always easy. But perhaps when it's hardest, it's most meaningful.

We are what He has made us, created in Christ Jesus for good works, which God prepared beforehand to be our way of life. (Ephesians 2:10)

Through Your grace, gracious God, may I find the strength to help the needy and poorly fed.

A Messenger of God's Love

Ask Sister Lisa Valentini whose life she'd pick if she could choose anyone's "in the whole wide world," and her answer will always be the same. "I'd pick mine every time," she says.

Her life has been mostly about missionary service, these days in the Dominican Republic. There, with two other Catholic Sisters in a small town north of Santo Domingo, Sister Lisa is the principal of two pre-schools, and also works with the parish youth group, choir and vocation promotion team.

"When I learned that there were more than a billion children who had never even heard the name 'Jesus,'" she explains, "something inside made me feel responsible to be a messenger of God's existence, of His love, to them—even in a small way."

We are all called to be "messengers of God's existence, of His love"—and that can start at home and in our community.

Love one another. Just as I have loved you, you also should love one another. By this everyone will know that you are My disciples. (John 13:34-35)

When You examine our lives, Father, may You not find us lacking in love and whole-souled respect for one another.

On Being Whole, Holy

A recent issue of *Body + Soul* Magazine offered suggestions for living which are worth effecting. Here they are:

- Happiness is not found in perfectionism.
- Healthy food is good for the environment and you.
- Your breath is a link between soul and body.
- Allow your body to move and stretch.
- Meditate. It's a natural instinct.
- Physical work is a pleasure. Rediscover that.
- Heed your body's signals when it feels out of balance.
- Ask if your habits support who you want to be.
- Inhabit every one of your life's moments.

Remember, true beauty is internal. It comes from energy, wellness, harmony and inner energy.

Better off poor, healthy, and fit than rich and afflicted in body. ...There is no wealth better than health of body, and no gladness above joy of heart. (Sirach 30:14,16)

Thank You, generous Creator, for the gift of life. May the way in which I live express my gratitude.

Love Doctor Finds New Prescription

What happens when a dating coach who has spent his career making matches falls in love with someone who isn't his type at all?

According to *Newsday,* Charley Wininger, the so-called "Love Doctor," thought he knew the most compatible kind of woman for him. Then he met her antithesis in Shelley Yeffet. While he's a psychotherapist interested in politics and questioning life's meaning, she's a gregarious registered nurse who sings show tunes in the shower.

After their first date Wininger felt confused. Then he had an epiphany: "I realized I was in love with her." Charmed by her bubbly ways, he proposed and they were married a few months later.

Wininger learned that "If you're not having fun at the beginning, you never will. To have that joyful bond, of play and celebration and fun, will get you through the bumps and the snags that invariably come."

How can you welcome more play-filled love into your life?

I am my beloved's and my beloved is mine. (Song of Solomon 6:3)

Loving God, my beloved teacher, teach me how to love.

Genuinely Pro-Life

A 13-year-old girl's room, heated by a space heater she couldn't control, had a urine soaked mattress, pillow, blanket and empty dresser; no toys, no books. A bare light bulb hung overhead.

The door was secured by an outside deadbolt lock and an alarm. A camera watched her. She had one minute bathroom breaks; left the room only for meals and chores. When she was late to meals, the girl wasn't allowed to eat and would have to steal scraps of food to assuage her hunger.

Her absence from school, church and neighborhood went unnoticed. When she began to hear voices, her folks brought her to an ER. They've been jailed for "causing mental harm to a child." Psychiatrists and the girl's maternal grandparents are trying to restore her mental health.

Work for an end to violence against people from the womb to the tomb. Pay attention to the welfare of vulnerable people in your neighborhood.

Jesus...said..."Whoever welcomes this child in My name welcomes Me, and...the One who sent Me; for the least among all of you is the greatest. (Luke 9:47-48)

Jesus, remind us that when a child is abused, it's You, the Son of God, who's abused.

Decide for Yourself

What do these three quotes have in common?

- "Everyone is born 'a somebody.' You choose whether to stay a somebody or not by how you act." —*Don McGee*

- "No one can make you feel inferior without your consent." —*Eleanor Roosevelt*

- "The truth is that there is nothing noble in being superior to somebody else. The only real nobility is in being superior to your former self." —*Whitney Young*

In fact, the writers were all talking about the same thing, our choices. What we make of our lives and how we think about ourselves in relation to other people is up to us. More than that, every day of our lives we get to make new choices about who and what we are and where we're going. God gave us our lives to make of them what we will.

Today, choose for yourself. Choose well.

Choose life so that so that you and your descendants may live. (Deuteronomy 30:19)

Author of life and love, endow me with Your wisdom that I may choose for myself all that is right and good and true.

The Ride to Build Houses

It took 30 college students two months to bike 4,000 miles from Providence, Rhode Island, to San Francisco. Several times they stopped to help construct homes with Habitat for Humanity.

In addition to fundraising for that organization, the students also hoped to encourage others to address the lack of affordable housing in the United States. More than 30 million individuals are without adequate housing in the U.S. where the median fair-market cost of a two-bedroom rental is more than 250% of federal minimum wage.

"Affordable housing is an issue we thought was important enough to commit a summer to," said cyclist Rachel Dearborn who attends Brown University, where 18 student riders were studying.

By the end of the experience, the cyclists had each raised $4,000 for the cause and made lasting friendships—all while helping others.

How can you insure affordable housing.

The thought of my...homeless is wormwood and gall!...But this I call to mind...the steadfast love of the Lord never ceases. (Lamentations 3:19,21,22)

Merciful God, inspire architects, city planners and builders to construct affordable housing.

Family Ties

Giovanni Cafiso, a barber, was a man torn between his family and, well, his family.

At age nine, he began a four-year barber's apprenticeship in Pozzallo, Sicily. He came to the U.S. when he was 21. For 45 years, six days a week, Cafiso cut his loyal customers' hair and discussed life with them. He accommodated their needs, arriving as early as 6:30a.m., leaving as late as 7p.m.

Then Cafiso and his wife needed to raise a granddaughter, Giovanna. Each winter, Rosa Cafiso and the little girl returned to their Sicilian homestead. Giovanni Cafiso stayed behind, barbering, sleeping at the back of his shop. Lonely, he started to think about and regret his absences when his own children were growing up.

Finally, he decided his family needed him more than his customers and he returned to Sicily.

Careers are important, but family much more so.

The wisdom of the humble lifts their heads high, and seats them among the great. (Sirach 11:1)

Bless grandparents, Ancient of Days.

In the Eye of the Beholder

While some see a restaurant's used-cooking oil as waste, Brent Arrow Baker sees it as potential clean diesel fuel.

This self-described "Johnny Appleseed" of biofuels is convinced that biodiesel technology will become "a major replacement of petroleum."

Baker's plan includes a refinery in Brooklyn, which will process vegetable grease from local restaurants into environmentally friendly fuel for diesel engines.

"We have a small fleet of vacuum trucks that will go to local restaurants and collect waste from cooking oil, which is what's known as a 'nuisance product' because it's often disposed of illegally down the drain," the 36-year-old entrepreneur told *The New York Times*. What's more, Baker's company will not charge restaurants for collecting the waste oil.

If there's a seemingly intractable problem, try to find a new way of looking at it.

The clever do all things intelligently. (Proverbs 13:16)

Inspire all of us, Holy Spirit, to make every effort to care for earth—Your gift to us and our home.

Motherly Love—Not Just for Children

19-year-old Lakenya Cannon needs guidance and care like any young adult. What makes Cannon's needs more pronounced is that she herself is the mother of a young son. That's where Loretha Weisinger comes in.

Part mentor, part coach and all-around helper and advocate, Weisinger served as Cannon's doula (combination midwife, coach and mentor) before, during and after the birth of Cannon's baby.

With four children and 13 grandchildren herself, Weisinger is no stranger to childbirth and child rearing. Beyond helping young mothers through birthing and parenting, she believes her work has great spiritual meaning. "The main thing that I think I'm doing is giving them their voice," she says, of her clients.

In fact, "mothering the mother" is often the main focus for doulas. Weisinger says that she is often the first nurturing presence in troubled lives.

Reach out to help a young person today.

You...took me from the womb; You kept me safe on my mother's breast. On You I was cast from my birth, and since my mother bore me You have been my God. (Psalm 22:9-10)

Divine Lord, bless young mothers with courage, strength and endurance.

Bryon and Bambo

Everyone knows the cliché that a man's best friend is his dog, but a deer? Bryon Davenport of Athens, Georgia, says his two best friends are his dog Levi and deer Bambo.

One day the car ahead of him struck and killed a doe. A scrawny shaky-legged fawn stood beside her corpse. After he drove home, Davenport, who considered himself a tough man, kept thinking about the fawn. So he returned, found it and brought it home. Levi welcomed the fawn by licking his face. A beautiful man-dog-deer friendship had begun.

Bambo grew up in Davenport's house, until he became full-grown. Davenport then found a research facility that would care for Bambo. But losing the deer finally enabled him to face the death of his father, his bad marriages and other losses. He visits Bambo every once in awhile, with peppermint, the deer's favorite treat.

Friends—human and otherwise—can help us to face our losses and heal.

Faithful friends are a sturdy shelter...a treasure... beyond price; no amount can balance their worth. (Sirach 6:14,15)

Bless us with faithful friends, Mighty One of Jacob.

New Testament Parenting Guide

When she became pregnant, Mary Curran Hackett read books on raising children and watched television shows with parenting experts. Soon she realized something or rather, Someone was missing: Jesus.

Hackett remembers her mother only using one book, the Bible. "My mother's Bible was marked with notes and filled with bookmarks holding pages that were undoubtedly special to her," Hackett notes. The Bible gave her "extra maternal motivation" whenever she needed help.

Some favorite New Testament passages are: The Beatitudes in Matthew 5:3-12; Matthew 6:25-34 on not worrying; Mark 10:13-16 which reminds us that Jesus respected and loved children; Luke 2:41-52 which shows us Jesus as a boy.

Experts offer some solutions to problems. But God is always there for us, always ready to lead us to the right choices and decisions.

Train children in the right way, and when old they will not stray. (Proverbs 22:6)

Gentle Jesus, remind parents that gentleness and respect are the ways to a child's heart and mind; in fact, Your ways.

A Day for Dining Out—Or Is It?

Mondays may not be the best time to go to a restaurant, according to a recent article in *The New York Times*. After the weekend, the best chefs might be taking a break.

In fact, that article suggested other "best times" not to do a lot of life's activities.

For example, since most hospitals are better staffed on weekdays than weekends, it's better for babies if they are fortunate enough to be delivered Mondays through Fridays. And if you're thinking of cleaning out your e-mail inbox, try Sunday afternoon. E-mail marketing experts say Mondays are bad because you are more likely to rush through the messages in a burst of resolution, often without carefully reading half of them.

But no matter the day of the week, it's always a good time to give thanks to God for His goodness and the good things He sends our way.

O give thanks to the God of heaven, for His steadfast love endures forever. (Psalm 136:26)

Yesterday, today and tomorrow, Father, You are light and hope for each day.

Moms Can Play Sports, Too

Athletes' mothers are often found on the sidelines watching their children play and screaming their support. But Paige Brodie decided, "We spend so much time watching these games, we should play ourselves." That was the beginning of a moms' soccer league in her town of Sherborn, Massachusetts.

When a mother plays the same sport as her children, it helps her to understand the challenges they face. One mother gives the example that she used to yell at her son to keep running during his games. Now that she plays, she realizes that running constantly is not an easy thing to do.

These moms also believe they are being good role models for their children. They are showing their children that age is not a factor in setting and reaching a goal you want.

It can be unnerving to try new things, but that shouldn't stop you from living life. Take risks. Make changes. Have fun.

As a mother comforts her child, so will I comfort you. (Isaiah 66:13)

Holy Wisdom, guide all Your people in living life fully, with risks, and with joy.

Unexpected Help

People see Rosa Murillo collecting cans and assume she's homeless. However, Murillo, an octogenarian who's a retired nanny, lives in a nice house with her former employer. She collects cans to raise money for missions in various countries.

Collecting cans is a way for Murillo to give back to those less fortunate than herself and to show her gratitude to God for her health. "I have letters from the missions and they say, 'Send money.' So I say 'Okay'," said Murillo, originally from Colombia, and now living in Troy, New York.

When she collects $200 or $300, she gives the money to a local priest who distributes it among missions, soup kitchens, and homeless shelters. Her hard work often results in $1000 a year.

Help comes in all shapes in sizes. Everyone has the potential to assist those in need. It only takes one person to light a candle.

You shall not watch your neighbor's donkey or ox fallen on the road and ignore it; you shall help to lift it up. (Deuteronomy 22:4)

Show us, Redeemer, who our neighbors are and how they need assistance.

Learning Is All Around Us

People who enjoy sports know that athletics can help us physically. Beyond that, they can be powerful teaching tools. Persistence, teamwork and dedication are a few of sports' benefits—and there are more.

"Baseball teaches us how to deal with failure," said former Commissioner of Baseball Fay Vincent. "We learn at a very early age that failure is the norm in baseball and, precisely because we have failed, we hold in high regard those who fail less often—those who hit safely in one out of three chances and become star players. I also find it fascinating that baseball alone in sports considers errors to be part of the game, part of its rigorous truth."

Whether sports, art, music, literature or other areas which offer us recreation, we can gain much more than pleasure and entertainment if we stay open to learning—wherever we find it.

From the fig tree learn its lesson. (Mark 13:28)

Blessed Trinity, help us to honor our bodies, minds and hearts by opening ourselves to Your wisdom wherever we find it.

Business Standards

Architect and urban redeveloper Guy Bazzani's Grand Rapids, Michigan, company restores old buildings with environmentally friendly techniques and tools. Judy Wicks buys all the produce for her White Dog Café in Philadelphia from local organic farmers.

Both belong to business networks that have sprung out of the Business Alliance for Local Living Economies, or Balle, an organization that promotes the concept that businesses can be simultaneously profitable and foster social and environmental awareness.

"We wanted to be a force to make businesses become positive role models," says Laury Hammel, the owner of a group of health clubs in the Boston area and a co-founder of Balle.

Says fellow co-founder Wicks, "We do well by doing good because we're known to do the right thing and people appreciate that."

Doing the right thing is always right.

Those who do not follow the advice of the wicked...but their delight is in the law of the Lord...are like trees planted by streams of water, which yield their fruit in its season. (Psalm 1:1,2,3)

Guide my steps, Master, as I labor to be aware of the impact of my decisions and actions.

Why Kids Can Do without Kid Gloves

Have society's well-meaning efforts to shield kids from harm gone too far?

A Pittsburgh, Pennsylvania, school refrained from using red pens to correct kids' homework because the color might seem too harsh. School authorities recommended that teachers use only "pleasant-feeling tones" when marking papers.

Or, consider the Santa Monica, California, school district that does not permit certain types of games, such as dodge-ball or tag, for fear of creating "self-esteem issues."

The intentions are well-meaning. But in an effort to protect youngsters' self-esteem, some parents and educators could be robbing them of vital lessons that help develop character and maturity. In addition, experts say that showering kids with undeserved praise may be associated with antisocial behavior.

Children need guidance, rules and limits, but they are also resilient. Sometimes, the best way to build character is to allow a child to learn through trial and error.

Keep these words that I am commanding you today in your heart. Recite them to your children. (Deuteronomy 6:6-7)

Holy Spirit, guide parents' efforts to raise well-rounded, good-hearted children.

Fixing Your Finances

What do knitters and financially prudent people have in common? "All knitters make mistakes. We know the smallest infraction at the beginning of a project can produce disastrous results if not corrected," writes Mary Hunt in *Woman's Day.*

Financial trouble doesn't usually happen overnight. "Rather it was a series of small, uncorrected mistakes that escalated over time," Hunt says. "The secret to staying out of the red is correcting those mistakes before they lead to disaster."

- If you spend each paycheck, skip restaurant dinners or cancel the gym and walk for a few months. Save a little.
- Using your home's equity as an ATM? It might be time to downsize to a more affordable house.
- Consider giving up the idea of a brand-new car with unsound loan terms for a more affordable used model.

We learn from mistakes and need not be afraid to admit them and move on.

All of us make many mistakes. (James 3:2)

Help us learn from our mistakes, Loving Lord.

Roses, in Memoriam

Gene Bliska recalls that his wife, Nancy, thought it was a shame to hoard the roses in their garden for themselves. Every week, she took two enormous bouquets to local nursing homes.

Bliska, whose wife died after 28 years of marriage and a 14 year struggle against breast cancer, says, "this garden is my way of celebrating Nancy. These roses keep her memory alive." He adds, "Tending our roses is my way of communicating with her. I think of my wife whenever I'm out there (with the roses)."

Today the Nancy Bliska Memorial Rose Garden in Greenwich, Connecticut, contains 1,400 rose plants on more than two acres.

One weekend a year it is open to the public. A company donates rosebushes which are sold and the proceeds are donated to the American Cancer Society's breast cancer research .

There are many ways to remember, celebrate and keep loved ones' memories alive which will also aid the living.

The memory of the righteous is a blessing. (Proverbs 10:7)

Ease the suffering of the grieving, Compassionate Savior.

"The Keeper of the Dream"

Verone Kennedy grew up in a rough New York City neighborhood where he saw friends die young. He had little interest in school, so it was no surprise that one of his teachers predicted he'd "end up dead or in jail."

What is a surprise is that Kennedy eventually became one of the city's most well-respected high-school principals.

Kennedy strives to provide a future for his students. "This world is so harsh to children. "I see myself as the keeper of the dream that is in every child, and I know we can succeed."

"These kids don't see themselves past 21," he says from first-hand experience. "I know that for them to see me here helps them believe that they can succeed."

Kennedy serves as a role model for those students, proving that, with clear goals and a positive outlook, anyone can succeed.

Do you know someone whose life needs direction?

Let us set an example. (Judith 8:24)

Help us teach and love others the way You did, Jesus.

Living and Loving Together

Most of us probably think we're good at relating to others, not only family and friends, but co-workers, neighbors and strangers. What about the folks who are different...who look or sound different than we do or who hold different beliefs?

"Into the world of fears and hatreds we need to pour a double portion of the spirit of confidence in the power of love," said Rev. Peter Green, an Anglican priest and writer. "Not peace at any price, but love at all cost. All our problems today resolve themselves into the problem of learning to live together."

How good a job are we doing at loving one another? There's not much point decrying the lack of tolerance, forgiveness and peace in the world if we don't develop tolerance, forgiveness and peace in our lives. God asks us to love not only the lovable, but those who–to us anyway–aren't. No exceptions.

Owe no one anything, except to love one another. (Romans 13:7)

God of Love, forgive my lack of love and enkindle Your own love for all Your children in my heart.

Argue the Wright Way

The Wright Brothers are well-known around the world for their invention of the airplane; it's less well known that the idea nearly stayed on the ground.

The brothers often argued about the craft to the point that their friends couldn't see how they could keep working together. But they learned to see both sides of the dispute.

"Honest argument is merely a process of mutually picking the beams and motes out of each other's eyes so both can see clearly," said Wilbur Wright.

One way that they devised to see the other's perspective was to switch their position during a quarrel.

"After I get hold of a truth, I hate to lose it again, and I like to sift all the truth out before I give up on an error," Wilbur Wright added.

The next time you face a disagreement, try to treat your opponents the way the Wright Brothers did—like family.

Why do you see the speck in your neighbor's eye, but do not notice the log in your own eye? (Matthew 7:3)

Nurture in us an appreciation for other people's viewpoints, Spirit of Counsel.

From Grief, Safety

In May, 2000, Abdul Hafiz lost his 16-month-old brother, Ibrahim, when the child crawled out a window of their Staten Island apartment and fell from a fifth-floor fire escape.

Devastated by the loss of his younger sibling, Hafiz teamed up with a teacher and some classmates. They gathered thousands of signatures petitioning for the installation of fire-escape window safety-gates. Abdul then helped lobby for a bill mandating the safety-gates for multifamily housing with children under age ten.

Abdul Hafiz's determination also led to a government grant which, in 2003, made possible the installment of fire-department-approved child safety gates in two housing developments in his own neighborhood.

By focusing our energy on a worthy cause, we can sometimes ease the pain of tragedy.

(Jesus) had compassion for her and said to her, "Do not weep." Then He...touched the bier, and...said, "Young man, I say to you, rise!" (Luke 7:13-14)

While we can not raise the dead to life, Jesus, please give us Your grace that we may imitate Your compassion for our family and friends.

What's Your Goal in Life?

A recent survey by the Higher Education Research Institute at the University of California at Los Angeles announced that 75 percent of young people aged 18 to 25 said it was "very important" to be "very well off financially."

The Pew Research Center conducted a poll for the same age group which shows 81 percent believe "getting rich is their generations most important or second-most important life goal."

The same Pew study also found that only 30 percent rated wanting to help people who need help first; 22 percent desired to be leaders in their own communities; 10 percent chose becoming more spiritual as their first goal.

People of all ages need to appreciate the value of money and all it can provide, while examining the deepest aspirations of their hearts.

What's most important to us? Would we answer the same on our dying day?

Lay up your treasure according to the commandments of the Most High, and it will profit you more than gold. Store up almsgiving...and it will rescue you from every disaster. (Sirach 29:11-12)

Divine Father, show me how to live my life by caring for my true needs of body, mind and spirit.

Life-Changing Songs

Nacho Pata looked at the issues affecting children in his native Mexico–and wrote songs about them.

The father of two young daughters is the lead singer of Los Patita de Perro (The Little Dog's Paw), a Mexican band for children that makes compelling music about the realities of young people's lives. "We think children are naturally intelligent and have no problems talking about the issues," Pata says.

The group has taken on violence, poverty and pollution, as well as corruption and commercialism. About the latter, he says, "Children don't need a lot of material things. They only want our love and our real attention."

In any language or place, the message of sharing love and attention is music to all our ears.

Let love be genuine. ...Love one another with mutual affection; outdo one another in showing honor. (Romans 12:9,10)

Jesus Christ, You took time to be present in love to all who came to You. Help me to imitate You.

"A Timeless Memory"

It's said that a picture is worth a thousand words. For the late Joe Rosenthal, the phrase could not be more appropriate.

Rosenthal photographed the world famous shot of U.S. soldiers hoisting a flag on Iwo Jima near the end of World War II.

"What I see beyond the photo is what it took to get up to those heights," Rosenthal said, "the kind of devotion to their country that those young men had, and the sacrifices they made."

At a time when Americans were weary of war, with families torn apart and the country disillusioned by the experience, the photo was a miracle, boosting the spirits of an entire country. *U.S. Camera* magazine said, "In that moment, Rosenthal's camera recorded the soul of a nation."

If a simple photograph has the power to bring hope to an entire country...what can you do to bring hope to the hopeless?

Hope deferred makes the heart sick. (Proverbs 13:12)

Compassionate God, enable me to find my limitless potential for bringing hope to others.

From a Chair to a Future

Kelee Katillac of Kansas City, Missouri, had a rough time in college and dropped out. Depressed and discouraged, she spent most of the day in her trailer.

One day, Katillac found a beat-up chair in the trash and took it home. Getting some fabric and paint from a thrift store, she went to work. Within days, she'd transformed the chair into something that made her proud.

Katillac got her old spark back and fixed up the rest of the trailer. She returned to school, then worked for a design firm before opening the House of Belief where she conducts workshops to help families, especially low-income ones, "make their homes an expression of what they believe."

She says, "It might sound crazy to you, but I believe God used that old chair to help heal me and give me a new purpose in life."

You never know where you may find God's plan for you.

Surely I know the plans I have for you, says the Lord, plans for your welfare and not for harm, to give you a future with hope. (Jeremiah 29:11)

Thank You, Abba, for caring about me, Your beloved child.

A Fisherman Named Peter

When Pietro Parravano was born, his aunt made him a baby blanket embroidered with his name and a boat—a symbol of St. Peter, his namesake.

But not until he had acquired a master's degree in science and taught did he become a professional fisherman. More than 25 years later, he still feels a spiritual connection to his calling to the sea. "The ocean is my church," he says.

He contemplates the mystery of the ocean, of the fish that come from the deep. But most of all, he says, "I will never let go of the incredible feeling that every fish I catch feeds people, nourishes them." This mission grounds him.

Parravano has also served on committees planning a sustainable future for fisheries and has been awarded the National Oceanic and Atmospheric Administration Environmental Hero Award.

What's your calling? How do you feed others?

Some went down to the sea in ships. ...The Lord...commanded and raised the stormy wind....He made the storm be still, and the waves of the sea were hushed.
(Psalm 107:23,24,25,29)

Creator, thank You for filling the waters with an astounding variety of life.

Grace in Action

Dick Grace's life changed forever the day he met Anthony Frazer. The owner of a successful California winery, Grace had donated wine for a benefit sponsored by Magic Moments, an organization that helps fulfill the dreams of gravely ill children. Anthony was one of those children.

"He turned all those values I had read so much about into reality for me," Grace recalls. "He simply radiated love."

So he and his wife Ann set up the Grace Family Vineyard Foundation, supporting projects for children around the world.

But Grace's contribution goes beyond money: he personally visits the projects helped, taking a hands-on approach. The children are his teachers, he'll tell you—and believing in the good that must be done is his motivation.

Each one of us can do something to make a difference. Perhaps you'll find your answer today.

What does the Lord require of you but to do justice, and to love kindness, and to walk humbly with your God? (Micah 6:8)

Lord, may my words and deeds reveal Your love to a world thirsting for love.

Appreciate the Sacrifices

"The whole place exploded. I felt like I was on fire. I crawled out...with metal embedded in my face, under my eye, in my neck, shoulders, arms, chest, stomach, hips, legs, feet. I spent the next six months in and out of hospitals. The VA rated me 60 percent disabled. I was 20 years old," writes Vietnam veteran Dave Lawrence.

In time, he joined the Vietnam Veterans Motorcycle Club which raises money for veterans' causes. At their annual Memorial Day ride in 2004 they visited Freedom Rock in Greenfield, Iowa, which a young local man paints annually to honor those who have served or are serving in war.

That's a good way to remember veterans. But our best 'thank you' to veterans and their families would be in Abraham Lincoln's words "to do all which may achieve and cherish a just and lasting peace...with all nations."

Blessed are the peacemakers, for they will be called children of God. (Matthew 5:9)

Jesus, remind us of our obligations to care for veterans and their families. May we never fail them.

Shelter Is a Haven

When you see the words "homeless shelter" you probably think of a place that's bleak but, that's not true of Wellspring House, a 17th-century farmhouse with a fireplace and organic garden.

For 25 years, it's offered hospitality to seven families at a time. The average stay at this Massachusetts refuge is six months. During that time the residents, called guests, are expected to seek long-term housing as well as work or training.

There are rules: Dinner is at 6:15; children are tucked in by 8 p.m.; no TV during the day. What sets Wellspring House apart is the concern of the people who run it. More than 600 families have passed through and many return to say "thanks."

One woman, now a teacher, who lived there while she was pregnant and escaping an abusive marriage, says, "I had nothing. They made me believe in myself."

Do what you can to help others believe in themselves.

Encourage one another and build up each other. (1 Thessalonians 5:11)

Show me how to aid those in need, Redeemer.

Wise Food Choices

In 2006, Rich Heffern and his wife vowed to try to eat only food available within a 100-mile circle of their home in Kansas City, Missouri.

Writing about their experiences, Heffern said they were helping save energy by supporting local farmers and not relying on goods shipped from across the country. "Local food tastes better. It's fresher, and it's safer."

The Hefferns decided on a multi-pronged approach. They rented a plot in their city's community garden, visited farmers' markets and arranged to have a local farmer deliver vegetables to them weekly.

Local eating "keeps us in touch with the passing seasons," Heffern says. "At the community garden we visit with the other growers. When one of us is away for a week, others water and weed. We pay each other with sweet corn and melons."

This is just one way to return the human and humane to every aspect of our lives. What's your first step?

I have given you every plant yielding seed...and every tree with seed in its fruit; you shall have them for food. (Genesis 1:29)

God of all, remind us that it is You who give us food and enable us to cultivate, harvest, store and prepare it.

Going Home to Live

If we get sick and go to the hospital we expect to be treated, cured and sent home to recuperate. Unfortunately, many poor youngsters in developing countries get worse and even die when they go home. For instance, a child who has been treated for pneumonia may go home to a leaky shack and to parents who have little money for food, let alone medicine.

That's why, in 1991, Dr. Vera Cordeiro started Saúde-Criança Renascer (Children's Health Reborn) to improve the health of children in impoverished areas of Brazil when they leave a hospital. Funded by donations and awards, volunteers and staff tailor individual assistance for children and their families that might include anything from counseling to vocational training to roof repair.

"There is no happiness for one person in this crazy world," says Dr. Cordeiro. "Everybody is connected."

Do your utmost to connect with those in need in your neighborhood.

A Samaritan woman came to draw water, and Jesus said to her, "Give me a drink."...Many Samaritans...believed in Him because of the woman' testimony. (John 4:7,39)

Beloved Lord, who's needy in my community?

Supporting a Child's Dreams

"I want to build a lemonade stand," 4-year-old Alex told her mother Liz Scott.

But Scott was worried because Alex had cancer. "Staying positive was hard," she wrote in *Guideposts*. She didn't want her daughter to be disappointed if things didn't work out. But Alex was persistent because she wanted to give any money she raised "to my hospital."

Soon publicity drew attention to Alex's fund-raising idea. Soon people from all over contributed to her project. Others set up their own lemonade stands to benefit pediatric cancer research.

Just two months after the plucky youngster died, "Alex reached her goal of one million dollars," her mother wrote.

Nurture a child's dreams. And work for cures for the diseases that can destroy their young lives.

The child is not dead but sleeping. (Mark 5:39)

Inspire researchers and physicians to find the causes and cures for pediatric cancers, Son of God.

Dear Alma Mater

Do you remember your old school song? If so, it might reflect how you felt as a student.

That was the case for graduates of Maryland's Wiley H. Bates High School when they returned for a celebration and could sing, "There's a school that I love so well; it's Bates, dear Bates."

These accomplished adults maintain a deep affection for Bates, described as "long the cultural bastion of black Annapolis." It was named for a self-educated former slave who left a legacy of learning, self-sufficiency and forbearance before his death in 1935.

Closed in 1981, the building was put on the National Register of Historic Places in 1994. Now Bates is being renovated into senior housing and a community center thanks to the financial and spiritual support of those who remember "Dear Bates," with affection.

Honor the past and work for the future.

Seek His presence continually. Remember the wonderful works He has done, His miracles, and the judgments He uttered.
(1 Chronicles 16:11-12)

Help us to remember the good those who have gone before us did through You. Let us do good in our day, Adoni.

Wedding Rituals

Ever wonder how the idea of honeymoons started? Why brides wear white? Or why a bouquet is tossed?

White wedding dresses became very popular after Queen Victoria's marriage to Crown Prince Albert in the 1850s.

The tradition of throwing a bouquet has been traced back to some areas of Europe during the 14th Century when people believed that having a piece of the bridal gown would bring good luck. But since a gown was in danger of being shredded, bouquets became a substitute.

The word honeymoon is said to have roots in a Norse word that means "wedding-night month." Honey might also refer to the practice of newlyweds drinking a daily cup of honeyed wine during their first month of marriage.

It's interesting to consider the origins of traditions and rituals that play a part in our lives.

You made Adam, and...his wife Eve as a helper and support....I now am taking this kinswoman of mine...with sincerity. Grant that she and I may find mercy and that we may grow old together. (Tobit 8:6,7)

Merciful Savior, bless couples with respect, mutual understanding and mutual forgiveness.

Genuine Justice

Statues of Justice outside courthouses show a somber blindfolded woman in Greco-Roman garb holding scales aloft, indicating that Justice is impartial. While the overwhelming majority of laws are also serious, there are exceptions that can only be considered odd, if not overbearing:

- In Alabama dressing as a nun, priest or rabbi or "minister of any religion" for Halloween is punishable by a fine or jail time.
- A Carmel, New York, law prohibits men from wearing mismatched jackets and trousers.
- In Chico, California, playing hopscotch, street hockey, "baseball or any other game"–is forbidden on any "sidewalk, lane or alley."
- A Palm Bay, Florida, law forbids dragging a "sled, person on roller skates, wagon (or) toy vehicle" behind a bike.

Do your best to eliminate pointless laws– and to support just ones.

Those who look into the perfect law, the law of liberty, and persevere...will be blessed in their doing. (James 1:25)

Divine Lawgiver, remind us and all who write laws that governments derive their "just powers from the consent of the governed."

Now Is the Time

Do you always tend to put things off? Procrastination can affect more than your daily to-do list. It can affect your whole life.

The late Elizabeth Kubler-Ross, psychiatrist and author of *On Death and Dying*, worked with many terminally ill patients and their families, learning about life as well as death.

"There are dreams of love, life and adventure in all of us," she wrote. "But we are also sadly filled with reasons why we shouldn't try. These reasons seem to protect us, but in truth they imprison us. They hold life at a distance. Life will be over sooner than we think. If we have bikes to ride and people to love, now is the time."

Now *is* the time. Putting off plans doesn't put off life. It moves on whether we're doing all the good things we want to do or not. Enjoy today—and use it well.

Remember your Creator in the days of your youth, before the...years draw near when you will say, "I have no pleasure in them." (Ecclesiastes 12:1)

You give me so many blessings, generous Lord. Guide me in using them well for my own sake and for the good of Your people.

A Passionate March

Bernice Sims is not your ordinary artist. This septuagenarian from Brewton, Alabama, has her work on a U.S. stamp. How? By painting scenes from the Civil Rights Movement.

"Those were bad times," says Bernice Sims. "It was such a hard struggle. For a long time, I thought that segregation was how life was always going to be."

Sims took part in the famous 1965 Bloody Sunday march, the inspiration for her stamp's image, called "Selma Bridge" It's part of a philatelic series called "To Form a More Perfect Union."

The events of that day turned her much-loved hobby into part of her passionate activism.

If you believe in something, do something. You'll never know the result until you try.

Those who do not love a brother or sister whom they have seen, cannot love God whom they have not seen. (1 John 4:20)

In our love for our fellow human beings and for You, Father, let us find the courage to stand up for our beliefs.

Expect the Unexpected

Watching fireflies, nighthawks and toads; listening for screech owls and whippoorwills; sitting in the grass stargazing. Few people would be surprised at having those experiences out in the country. But in New York City?!

Nevertheless, city dwellers are being introduced to the wonders of the skies and splendors of nature through special overnight programs offered by the New York City Department of Parks and Recreation.

"There's nothing more magical than being in the park on a summer night," said Adrian Benepe, N.Y.C. Parks Commissioner, "with the breeze and the sound of crickets and the cicadas, and the birds going to bed."

Appreciate God's creation. And, stay open to life's unexpected possibilities.

God...determines the numbers of the stars...covers the heavens with clouds, prepares rain for the earth, makes grass grow on the hills....He gives snow like wool; he scatters frost like ashes...hail like crumbs. (Psalm 147:1,4,8,16,17)

Lord of beauty and strength, in Nature's beauty and strength may we see flashes of Your own.

Raising Your Teens

As teens have more social activities, parents worry about their safety. Dr. Ray Guarendi, a psychologist who writes about childrearing, says a woman told him her system for supervising her teens. Before they went out, they had to answer the five W's: Who? What? Where? When? Why?

- Who will be with you? Know, really know, your children's friends and their friends' parents.

- What will you be doing? Let youngsters know that any change in plans must be cleared first.

- Where are you going? Some places are probably off-limits.

- When will you be home? You may be answering this one yourself.

- Why are you going? Make sure there are no hidden agendas, like meeting other teens you don't want yours to be with.

Remind teens that all these are related. One unacceptable response could negate the others. Above all, encourage your children's good judgment and character by example.

The Lord honors a father above his children, and He confirms a mother's right over her children. (Sirach 3:2)

Beloved Father, help me live my life to honor You and to grow in faith, hope and love.

The Value of Friends

Without Paula Ferry-Wineck, at whose wedding he had been the best man, Kim Connors might not have come to grips with the terminal disease that threatened him.

Married with two sons, Connors was diagnosed with ALS, or Lou Gehrig's disease. Soon he had to live in a long-term care hospital and had to communicate via a laptop computer.

Then his wife, Liz Connors, was killed in a freak accident. Kim Connors had become a single father. His friend Ferry-Wineck stepped in, bringing the grieving, discouraged Connors a listening, encouraging presence.

Realizing that his sons needed him, Connors returned home with the help of a caretaker and a housekeeper. Ferry-Wineck brought him home cooked meals and continuing inspiration. In turn, Connors became the father his sons needed, even going to their basketball and hockey games

Each day, we have the chance to show God's love to others. Today celebrate life!

The Lord is the stronghold of my life. (Psalm 27:1)

Redeemer, guide us in reaching out to others who need our love — Your love — in so many ways.

A Sense of Vocation

When was the last time you considered the mission to which God has called you? Here are some thoughts from Greg Pierce, writing in *Lutheran Women Today* magazine.

"Would we act differently if we were convinced that what we do every day was a call from God? Would we see the meaning of what we do differently? God's work never ends. Creation is an ongoing labor throughout time. It includes peak moments and tedious daily tasks. Co-workers, even competitors, can be opportunities of grace, rather than obstacles to be overcome.

"If we had a sense of vocation, we would balance the various responsibilities in our life – job, family, community and church. To think that there would be even one child of God who is not called to something important, would be to underestimate God's interest in and concern for each of us."

What is God asking of you?

Before I formed you in the womb I knew you, and before you were born I consecrated you...a prophet to the nations. (Jeremiah 1:5)

Holy Spirit, what are You calling me to do today?

Volunteering as a Way of Life

It's never too early for public-spirited parents to nurture the volunteer spirit in their children. "Studies have shown that volunteering is a learned behavior," writes John Hanc. "So I figured it was time for my 11-year-old son to put down his PlayStation and start learning."

Father and son explored various volunteer options and settled on "a cross section of causes—the environment, animals and a soup kitchen. All of them inspired us to want to come back and keep helping in the future," notes Hanc.

According to a spokesperson for Volunteers of America, family volunteering is on the rise. The experience ought to be rewarding for the child, not something parents force them to do. "People should volunteer where they and their children have an interest or passion."

Many non-profit groups, schools and faith communities offer opportunities. Volunteer as a family.

From my youth You have taught me.
(Psalm 71:17)

Inspire families to help the needy together, Father.

First Lady Hero

Many associate Dolley Madison, wife of U.S. President James Madison, with grand parties. Indeed, this First Lady whom the press called "Queen Dolley" decorated the White House and held weekly gatherings at which Congressmen, foreign diplomats and celebrities mingled.

But in the summer of 1814, with the British army approaching Washington, D.C., and her husband gone to address troops, she received word that the American army was in retreat. Dolley Madison took action. She loaded secret papers into trunks and even secured a large portrait of George Washington, finally fleeing to safety.

British troops did burn down the White House and the U.S. Capitol before returning to their ships. But when the White House was rebuilt a few years later, Washington's portrait was–thanks to Dolley Madison–returned to its rightful place.

Our actions, big or small, make a difference.

Deborah, a prophetess...was judging Israel... (she) summoned Barak...and said to him...'take position at Mount Tabor bringing ten thousand (soldiers)'...(God) will draw out Sisera. (Judges 4:4,6,7)

Almighty God, be with me so that I may act courageously all the time.

"My Dad...Father of The Century"

"Dad, when we were running, it felt like I wasn't disabled anymore." Those words, typed on a specially adapted computer, started Rick Hoyt and his father Dick on a previously unimaginable journey.

Told their son was "a vegetable"–he had been strangled by his umbilical cord during birth–Dick and Judy Hoyt proved otherwise. In high school, Rick wanted to participate in a charity fundraising race. His then out-of-shape father pushed him in his wheelchair for five miles. After that, Dick Hoyt got into shape so they could compete.

The two have entered and completed marathons and triathlons. Dick Hoyt pushes the wheelchair, tows Rick Hoyt in a dingy while swimming, and pedals with him on the handlebars.

Rick Hoyt is able to live independently (with home care) though he and his father find ways to be together. He says, "No question about it, my dad is the Father of the Century."

Every child needs hope-filled parental love.

Everyone who loves is born of God and knows God. (1 John 4:7)

Creator, You know we are all handicapped in some way. Help us, therefore, to love each other into wholeness.

"Achieving Happiness"

Chris Gardner defines success as "looking in the mirror and saying 'I like this guy'."

After growing up poor and living in foster homes, he started a family with his girlfriend. His girlfriend then left him with their son. He did not have a job and needed to provide for himself and his little boy.

Gardner talked his way into Dean Witter's broker training program, but the program's small stipend couldn't pay for day care, food, and shelter. So the two often went without shelter, sleeping in subway station restrooms.

But Gardner's gamble paid off: he was hired by the company. And, eventually, he started his own brokerage firm.

Now a multimillionaire with a best-selling memoir and a feature film about his life (*The Pursuit of Happyness*), Gardner is able to look in the mirror every morning and like what he sees.

Can you look in the mirror and do the same?

**I took you from the pasture, from following the sheep to be prince over My people.
(2 Samuel 7:8)**

Caring God, remind me that in Your presence my struggles can strengthen me to be and do great things.

Father Joe's House of Hope

Klong Toey, one of Thailand's forgotten communities, offers little hope in its desperate living conditions, slums and crime-ridden streets and alleys.

Yet, Father Joe Maier, a Redemptorist priest who lives and works there, has found a way to give hope to the city's destitute, ill and abandoned.

Maier's 30-year campaign to bring decency and compassion to the suffering that dominates Klong Toey is embodied in Mercy Center. This is a comprehensive resource that includes four orphanages, a shelter for street children, a home for mothers and children with HIV/AIDS, and a primary school.

Despite the seemingly unending illness and poverty around him, Maier says, "This is a sacred place. All of this is in the hands of God, who will point us always in the proper direction."

Hope can be found in the direst of circumstances. The effort of one single human being is enough to launch hope enough for many.

Hope does not disappoint us. (Romans 5:5)

Merciful Jesus, Your earthly life serves as a foundation of hope for us all.

When Sweet 16 Turns Sour

A young girl's "Sweet 16" celebration used to consist of an at-home party or sleepover, with a few presents and a focus on her moving toward adulthood.

Today, thanks to commercial marketing, a new level of affluence and peer pressure, teens are demanding and expecting more. Some want lavish, catered parties as well as cars and vacations as "gifts." Has the trend gone too far?

Karen Quinn believes it has. When her 14-year old daughter began to plan a catered event at a major hotel for her Sweet 16 celebration, Quinn put on the brakes, and simply said no.

Experts suggest these tactics to discourage teens' unrealistic expectations:

- Insist that your children earn what they get.
- Set spending limits even on so-called essentials.
- Don't be afraid to say no.

It's up to adults to model adult behavior. That means living with limits and responsibilities.

Train children in the right way, and when old, they will not stray. (Proverbs 22:6)

Divine Master, help parents teach their children to resist overindulgence and to enjoy life with adult obligations.

Giving Back

Karen Borchert and Jessica Jackson started Campus Kitchens Program (CKP) after they graduated from Wake Forest University. As juniors, they had realized that the homeless needed decent meals. They started cooking for people whom Durham, North Carolina's First Presbyterian Church identified as needy. Other students volunteered to help. At their graduation, over 400 meals a month were being prepared.

Running CKP takes work. The women ask for donations of food, contact agencies to find needy people, raise money and, of course, prepare food. A volunteer said, "This program is unique because it creates a support system for the needy." There are currently six CKPs on campuses throughout the country.

College campuses prepare so much food that leftovers are guaranteed. If all institutions gave their leftovers to the needy, many hungry people could be helped.

It is more blessed to give than to receive. (Acts 20:35)

Show us how to use well Your gift of abundant food, Lord of the Harvest.

"Dream to Differ"

Many are unsatisfied with their jobs, wishing they could do something more enjoyable. Though it may seem like a dream, it's possible to turn your biggest passion into a career opportunity.

Julie Baggenstoss was a television news producer. The uncontrollable schedule bothered her. She turned to what made her happy–flamenco dancing–and is now a dance instructor at Emory University.

Vince Stanton worked at a tire shop for years before taking a chance on his dream. He now makes over $100,000 in prizes annually as a professional bull rider.

Co-founder of Cisco Systems Sandy Lerner quit her job to become an organic farmer.

Remember, the best job is the job to which you enjoy going. And, the only thing that can stop you from doing what you want is yourself. How can you turn your dream into a career?

Who can stand before (Leviathan)? Who can confront it and be safe?–under the whole heaven, who? (Job 41:10-11)

Redeemer, help us dare to confront our fears and achieve our dreams.

Summertime is Here

Summer begins with the summer solstice between June 21st and 23rd. On this day, "the sun appears to 'stand still' in the sky."

Courtney Hargrave, writing in *Woman's Day*, defines heat as "the sensation or perception of such energy as warmth or hotness; a hot season; a spell of hot weather." She also provides some additional thoughts on heat:

- The hottest recorded temperature in North America was 134°F in Death Valley, California.

- The melting point for a diamond is 6,416.33 degrees Fahrenheit, higher than any other mineral.

- Standing in direct sunlight can make it feel 15 degrees hotter than it really is.

David Weatherford said, "We enjoy warmth because we have been cold. We appreciate light because we have been in darkness. By the same token, we can experience joy because we have known sadness."

Enjoy the sun's warmth. Enjoy God's gifts.

The sun...runs its course with joy. Its rising is from the end of the heavens, and its circuit to the end of them; and nothing is hid from its heat. (Psalm 19:4,5-6)

Thank You, Generous Creator, for the joyfulness which a sunny day imparts.

The Fruits of Fenway Park

Most people know Fenway Park as the home of the Boston Red Sox. But did you know that a nearby seven-acre plot, known as Fenway Gardens, is home to the last victory garden in the United States?

During World War II, civilian food rationing and shortages prompted President Franklin D. Roosevelt to ask citizens to grow their own food. Government, schools and businesses worked to get land and teach people how to farm. Hence Fenway Gardens became an original victory garden.

Today, Fenway Gardens is thriving, with over 300 gardeners, who pay $30 per plot. What they grow is as varied as the gardeners themselves: Carmen Musto, fruit trees; restaurateur Leo Romero, herbs and flowers; Phyllis Hanes, unusual vegetables from seed.

To connect with the earth through gardening or conservation enhances our relationship with God and improves our planet.

God said, "Let the earth put forth vegetation. ...And it was so. ...And God saw that it was good. (Genesis 1:11,12)

Spirit of Life, help us connect with You; with the Earth; with all that's dearest, truest, deepest within ourselves.

Meaning What You Say

Parents know their obligations to provide for the welfare of their children. Beyond the basics of food, clothing and shelter are others such as education and medical care. And then there's the need to help develop character.

"If you haven't noticed, kids are great moral philosophers, especially as they get into adolescence," says Jim Rohm, author of *Cultivating an Unshakable Character.* "They're determined to discover and expose any kind of hypocrisy, phoniness, or lack of integrity on the part of authority figures, and if we're parents, that means us. It really isn't a conscious decision on their part; it's just a necessary phase of growing up.

"They're testing everything, especially their parents. This is a great opportunity and also a supreme responsibility, because kids simply must be taught to tell the truth: to mean what they say and to say what they mean."

Teach with your words and your example.

If you...know how to give good gifts to your children, how much more will the heavenly Father give the Holy Spirit to those who ask him! (Luke 11:13)

Parents and children need Your care and guidance, Beloved Father. Aid us in helping one another.

Helping Others Sing Like Angels

With her diminutive stature, Ite O'Donovan hardly looks like the type of person who can silence a room with a few taps. Yet, she does exactly that, as conductor of the Dublin Choral Foundation.

In existence for roughly a decade, the Foundation is supported in part by commercial backers, with no government or religious affiliation. Yet, its in-depth training program is regarded as a coveted training ground for young singers, particularly due to the talent and effort of O'Donovan.

One of the most appealing aspects of the choir is that it mixes ages and sexes so successfully its vocal possibilities and enjoyment often surpass those of more traditional choirs.

Diversity brings more than just variety. The richness of a diverse setting yields benefits not apparent on face value alone.

Act with justice and righteousness, and deliver from the...oppressor...the alien, the orphan, and the widow. (Jeremiah 22:3)

Enrich our lives, Jesus, with the opportunity to appreciate other cultures, creeds, races and nationalities.

365 Days of Christmas

Who says we can't have Christmas spirit all year long?

If we try to spread some of our December cheer and good will throughout the other eleven months, we'll not only do good for others, but feel pretty good ourselves. Try these ideas:

- Surprise a co-worker with a cup of coffee, or a neighbor by running an errand.
- Stay in touch with family and friends with notes, e-mails or photos.
- Think about crafts, like knitting or painting, that you can start working on now for gifts next Christmas.
- The toy and food drives you supported during the holidays could use your contributions throughout the year.
- Rent a Christmas-themed movie for the family to enjoy, like *A Christmas Carol, Miracle on 34th Street* or *It's a Wonderful Life.*

The spirit of Christmas is always within us—if we just believe and if we share.

**A generous person will be enriched.
(Proverbs 11:25)**

Child of Bethlehem, open my heart. Show me how to give and to receive with joy.

A Class Project

When Rita Neumeister's high school students started researching topics for debate, one made a startling discovery.

"Do you know how many kids are orphaned because of AIDS?" the teen said. "We have to do something."

The California high schoolers, along with Neumeister, decided to address the problem currently affecting more than 12 million children in Africa. They partnered with HERO, an organization that raises money for 37 schools in four African countries with a high proportion of AIDS orphans. Funds go toward the basics like food, clean water, and medical care. Selling handmade wristbands and T-shirts, the students raised $1,000 for KwaMaduma Junior Primary School in South Africa.

"If you put your mind to it, you can really change people's lives," said 16-year-old Alana Dowden of the class project. "You can make a difference."

With hope and faith in action, we can cope with any of life's challenges.

Just as the body without the spirit is dead, so faith without works is also dead. (James 2:26)

I hear Your cry for help through the poor and suffering, Lord. Show me how to answer You.

The Nun in Tennis Shoes

Say the name Andrea Yeager and most folks picture a teenage tennis sensation.

But today, the tennis skirts have been replaced by a black nun's habit—and now Sister Andrea, a Dominican Episcopal nun, runs a camp for kids with life-threatening illnesses on a ranch outside of Durango, California.

It was an encounter with a sick child when she was a 15-year-old tennis star that started her on this journey. "I felt like God was saying to me, 'When you grow up, you're going to help kids stuck in the hospital,'" she recalls.

"I've always seen God as my friend," she explains, adding that she looks for God's guidance in big and little decisions.

The bigger decisions included putting the $1.4 million she'd earned into her efforts for children.

"God knows the bigger picture," says Sister Andrea. "If you put your faith in Him that will produce the love, the tolerance, and the strength to help others."

Amen to that.

Cast your burden on the Lord, and He will sustain you. (Psalm 55:22)

Redeemer, show me Your ways.

Each for the Other

Every heritage offers wonderful traditions for the important events of life: birth, death, marriage. Special language and ceremonies handed down through the generations offer wisdom and celebration.

Here are the words of an Apache wedding blessing that has meaning for all newlyweds:

"Now you will feel no rain, for each of you will be shelter for the other.

"Now you will feel no cold, for each of you will be warmth for the other.

"Now there will be no more loneliness, for each of you will be companion to the other.

"Now you are two persons, but there is only one life before you.

"May your days together be good and long upon the earth."

May married couples everywhere grow continually in respect and joy at their one life together.

What God has joined together, let no one separate. (Mark 10:9)

Loving Lord, bless each and every bride and groom and may their days "be good and long upon the earth."

Into the Fire

Imagine someone saving a woman from a burning building. It's the typical hero story that one hears about on the evening news. Now imagine a blind man saving a blind woman from a burning building. Jim Sherman did just that.

Out of work and blind, Sherman was feeling worthless. When his neighbor asked him if he would listen to her mother, who was also blind, via a baby monitor to ensure her safety while the daughter was at work, he agreed.

One night after checking up on the woman, he turned in for the night, but was startled by a strange sound on the monitor. The sound gave way to a crash and he knew it was trouble.

So Sherman rushed to the house and miraculously found the scared woman and brought her to safety. Though the house was destroyed, Sherman and his neighbor escaped unharmed.

"Thank you, Lord," Sherman said, "for giving me a chance to help."

We all need to be needed.

Because you have made...the Most High your dwelling place...He will command His angels... to guard you in all your ways. (Psalm 91:9,11)

Send Your angels to us, God of Heaven and earth.

Turning No-thing into Some-thing

"There was nothing. No church structure. We started from zero."

This is how Bishop Wens Padilla describes his arrival in Mongolia in 1992. He led a small team of missionaries whose goal was to establish the Catholic Church's presence there.

Bishop Padilla and the missionaries found fertile ground: from a population of zero, the Catholic faith now numbers roughly 300 members in predominantly Buddhist Mongolia.

What's more, the original team of three missionaries has also grown, and spends most of its efforts providing housing, food and support for orphaned children.

Starting from scratch is never easy. It can even be discouraging. And, it may seem as though one's efforts are hopeless. Those who persevere rely on faith–that their efforts will indeed amount to something; that they are not alone.

They went out and proclaimed the good news everywhere. (Mark 16:20)

Empower me in the face of discouragement, Heavenly Father.

Giving Thanks Year-Round

Newsweek columnist Jayne Steiner-Kanak attempted to make every moment of her mother's life count during her battle with terminal emphysema.

Fearing that her mom would not live until the holidays, Steiner-Kanak decided to have Thanksgiving in July, letting her mother plan the menu, shopping lists, and decorations, all while supervising from her bed

"My mother always told us, 'Food is love,' and I was on a mission to show her how much I loved her," said Steiner-Kanak.

"Even as Mom's condition worsened, she remained very engaged in the process," said Steiner-Kanak. "We felt secure in the knowledge that she had thoroughly enjoyed her favorite time of the year that summer."

Thanksgiving may be one day of the year, but its ideals are timeless. Contemplate everything for which you are grateful, not only today but every day–whether it be friends, family, or even eating turkey in July.

**Offer to God a sacrifice of thanksgiving.
(Psalm 50:140)**

Thank You, Lord, for all You have given us.

Looking on the Bright Side

Don Karkos is used to injuries, as the blindness in his right eye from a World War II shrapnel explosion proved.

When the Monticello Raceway paddock security guard was head butted by a racehorse, he thought it was just another bump in a career of bruises. "Being kicked is part of the job, but I've never been hit that hard," said Karkos.

Little did Karkos know that the bump would solve his 60-year problem–it restored the vision in his eye. "It was unbelievable," Karkos said. "I've been seeing doctors all my life, and they've always told me there's nothing that can be done."

Karkos' story is proof that even long term problems can be solved.

Especially when things seem to be going poorly, it is important to remain positive; there may be a light at the end of the tunnel.

(Jesus) saw a man blind from birth...He spat on the ground and made mud with the saliva and spread the mud on the man's eyes, saying to him, "Go, wash"...(the man) came back able to see. (John 9:1,6-7)

May we always look toward You in times of darkness, Jesus.

Collecting Change to Break Chains

"I'm Zach and I am an abolitionist."

That's the message of 15-year-old Zach Hunter, who started "Loose Change to Loosen Chains" to support organizations that fight the global slavery of millions of adults and children.

Hunter travels throughout the United States talking with young people about the issue, painting a clear picture of the situation. "What if your feet were shackled together all day long as you sit on a dirt floor rolling cigarettes?" he asks. "What if you crushed boulders into gravel with a heavy hammer all day long until you were breathless, sun burnt and bleeding?"

The Virginia teen plans to meet with his Congressional representatives and to engage local business leaders in the movement to end slavery.

"If we all work together we can make a difference," Hunter believes. He's right.

By working with others, we can help end the enslavement of our fellow human beings.

You shall not deprive a resident alien or an orphan of justice...Remember that you were a slave in Egypt and the Lord your God redeemed you. (Deuteronomy 24:17-18)

Alert me to the innate dignity of all human beings, regardless of race, creed, nationality or gender, Liberator.

A Colonial Hero

"I only regret that I have but one life to lose for my country."

Those famous words were spoken by teacher and American spy Nathan Hale just before he was hanged without trial by the British in 1776. They have come down to us as an expression of genuine patriotism.

"He's a great example of a young American willing to give his best," said Stephen Shaw, property steward of the Connecticut Society of the Sons of the American Revolution. The society plans to turn each schoolhouse where he taught into a museum.

Robert G. Carroon, the organization's president said that "we are called upon to ensure that his memory and the principles for which he stood are made known to all generations."

In fact, we are called to defend that experiment in representative government for which Hale and so many others died. Be ready and willing to fulfill your obligations as a citizen.

Those who look into the perfect law...of liberty, and persevere, being not hearers who forget but doers who act – they will be blessed in their doing. (James 1:25)

Lord, remind us that justice and democracy must be defended every day.

Jumping Jacks for Your Brain

When was the last time your mind got a workout? Keeping your brain fit has a very real, measurable effect on everything you do. So, try these "exercises for the mind."

- **Get physical.** Exercising and eating healthfully are key to good health, including mental well-being. Make time for rest and relaxation as well.

- **Stay connected.** Be involved with others. Try to do a mentally stimulating activity like a crossword puzzle daily. Reduce more passive activities like television viewing.

- **Stop the stress.** With technology—e-mail, Internet, cell phones, blackberries—taxing us 24/7, we need to free ourselves from a frantic, frenzied, and frustrated state of mind. Ditch distractions and slow down to keep your wits about you.

In the final analysis, our minds and hearts are always healthier when filled with the hope of God's great love.

God is our refuge and strength, a very present help in trouble. (Psalm 46:1)

Slow me down, Divine Master, so that I may better experience Your goodness in my life.

Every Little Bit Helps

Elise Tierney and Rosemary Hanley were Missouri soccer moms who became friendly while watching their sons play. They volunteered with a local coat drive and in four years, collected 2,000 coats. Then they got a challenging call.

A St. Louis teacher said she had children coming to school without coats who were blue from the cold. The women gave out 170 coats that day and soon started the Little Bit Foundation to supply coats, jackets, hats and gloves to children whose families couldn't afford them.

Dan Buck, the head of a local agency helping people in need, says, "The work of these two ladies is an example of how a couple of friends can make an impact on thousands."

Tierney simply puts it this way: "God is so cool to let us do this. It's His work, not ours."

God can work wonders through each of us, if we let Him.

Has the Lord as great delight in burnt offerings and sacrifices, as in obeying the voice of the Lord? Surely, to obey is better than sacrifice, and to heed than the fat of rams.
(1 Samuel 15:22)

Your people are waiting for us to make a difference together, Compassionate Lord. Show us the way.

Honey Money

Farouk Jiwa wanted to help Kenya's poorest farmers, who own little land. Solution: bees!

Beehives don't need lots of space. Bees feed themselves, which means low costs for beekeepers to run their businesses. And they pollinate crops, which helps agricultural production.

So Jiwa co-founded Honey Care Africa, a company that trains subsistence farmers in beekeeping and guarantees them a market for their honey at fair-trade prices.

In a country where half the population lives on less than 50 cents a day, Jiwa's company is making a difference in the lives of thousands. Honey Care's 2,750 beekeepers, most of whom are women, use their honey money to buy food, medicine, schoolbooks for their children, seeds and fertilizers, or to make home repairs.

Nature, with a little nurturing from caring humans, can begin to solve a world of problems.

Eat honey, for it is good, and the drippings of the honeycomb are sweet to your taste. Know that wisdom is such to your soul; if you find it, you will find a future. (Proverbs 24:13-14)

Lavish sweet Wisdom on us, Holy Spirit.

Why a Volunteer?

Take any gathering of people, ask, "Who wants to volunteer?"–and you're likely to find almost everyone avoiding eye contact with the person uttering those words.

But, according to Brian Doyle, who learned a great deal from his volunteer stint as a religious education teacher, there are good reasons to give away your time–and talent–for free.

Doyle found the experience helped him learn new things, make new friends, and better experience his parish community. Not only that, he felt he was setting an example for others and helping to implement positive change.

But the best reason of all? "To enjoy yourself," Doyle says. "It may be difficult to remember after making 50 sub sandwiches for hungry kids, but you really can receive great satisfaction from helping others."

We are called to be God's love in the world every day, and some days that means raising–and lending–a helping hand.

To each is given the manifestation of the Spirit for the common good. (1 Corinthians 12:7)

Father, how can I bring Your love to others today?

What's Best for the Children?

Traditional solutions to a problem aren't always the best.

When parents cannot cope, children are often placed in foster care. But with the "shared-family-care" model, parents and children are relocated together to the home of a trained mentor. There parents learn by example and practice good child-rearing techniques.

One California mother, a "meth" addict, who had been unable to manage a home or care for her first seven children, got another chance with her youngest. Once she was in drug rehab, her mentor showed her proven ways to discipline, guide and love a child.

She says of her mentor, she "didn't make me feel like, 'You had eight kids–you ought to know.' So I just listened to her. I never had anyone that cared…that just cared."

All of these services and supports cost more initially. But when successful, this model breaks the cycle of abuse and neglect.

The Lord…confirms a mother's right over her children. (Sirach 3:2)

Make support for mothers a priority in our society, Lord.

Some Inspirational Sayings

Lauren Wiener compiled a list of thoughts by which to live for *Family Circle* magazine. Here are some of them:

- Think big thoughts but relish small pleasures. H. Jackson Brown Jr.

- My favorite thing is to go where I've never been. Diane Arbus

- There are only two ways to live life…as though nothing is a miracle …(or) as though everything is a miracle. Albert Einstein

- Think of all the beauty still left around you and be happy. Anne Frank

- The more you praise and celebrate your life, the more there is in life to celebrate. Oprah Winfrey

Regardless of the sayings you choose to live by, do not hold back or be afraid to make mistakes. Take chances. Make changes. Live life and enjoy every moment lest you waste it.

Live in love, as Christ loved us. (Ephesians 5:2)

My life is Your gift to me, Generous Creator. Enable me to embrace, celebrate and live my life to its fullest.

A Flair for Fair Trade

When Safia Minney was 25 and living in Japan, little did she know that her desire to be a conscientious consumer would result in a multi-million-dollar global business promoting fair trade and environmentally friendly products.

While in Tokyo, Minney's pursuit of organic food and environmentally friendly products prompted her to begin distributing leaflets on the subject. "I was a concerned consumer and I wanted to get a hold of those products anyway," she remembers.

Soon after, she launched an environmental-consumer organization from her home. Eventually, she had nearly 20 employees. The company soon expanded into several divisions, and eventually, Global Village, her flagship effort, was selling organic, fair-trade products around the world. A portion of her company's profits are used to support social projects around the world.

What sparks your inner spirit? Your own interests could translate into a new and unique way to help others.

In everything do to others as you would have them do to you; for this is the Law and the Prophets. (Matthew 7:12)

Caring Father, help me become more mindful of social justice in everything I do.

Releasing Shame

Sherry Grace of Orlando, Florida, lived a life of outward respectability. But, "my sons were my dirty little secret," she now admits. As teens, Andre and Avery ran around with the wrong crowd–and, over the years, ended up in and out of jail.

One day in 2000, Grace finally unburdened herself to members of her church. "I told them my sons had broken the law and were in prison," she recalls. Afterwards she felt better.

Realizing that those in similar situations also needed practical help and the chance to talk things over with others who understood, she founded Mothers of Incarcerated Sons. Since then, the nonprofit organization has helped 1,300 mothers of inmates in 23 states.

"People tend to think that someone is a failure when he goes to jail, but that's the wrong attitude," says Grace. "Failure is temporary."

Whether looking at yourself or others, never see just a "failure."

Help the weak, be patient. ...See that none of you repays evil for evil, but always seek to do good to one another and to all.
(1 Thessalonians 5:14,15)

Wrapped in Your love, Jesus, I am free of fear and full of hope!

Do Some Good Today

Gary Pranzo worked at an advertising agency for 40 years and "loved every minute of it." Yet, when he retired he found something that he says he gets "100 times more" from: volunteering.

For the last 12 years, along with Rose, his wife of 51 years, he's spent one day a week at Manhattan's Holy Apostles Soup Kitchen, the country's largest, feeding the hungry and homeless. They love their time together at the well-known Episcopal Church ministry with other volunteers who serve an average of 1,000 meals a day, 365 days a year.

When the Pranzos leave, they make a point of turning to each other and saying, "We did some good today."

There's no doubt that our work is important. That's how we make a living, after all. But, how we make a life involves the time and attention we give to family, friends, and, yes, strangers in need. Let's do all we can.

Clothe yourselves with compassion, kindness, humility, meekness, and patience. (Colossians 3:12)

Show me how You want me to serve Your beloved people, my sisters and brothers, Compassionate Lord.

Swords Into Plowshares—and Art

While violence, cruelty and brutality are all too obvious in our world, there are people everywhere who still seek to create, not destroy.

In Mozambique, a nonprofit called Transforming Arms into Tools encourages people to turn in weapons, many left from a civil war. In exchange, they receive useful items such as tools, building materials, bikes and sewing machines.

In addition, an artist named Kester, part of a collective called Nucleo de Arte, has used some of those weapons to create sculptures. These include *Tree of Life* and *Throne of Weapons,* made from rifles and AK-47s, which have gone on tour to call attention to peace-making efforts.

Meanwhile in Laos, Lee Moua, a Hmong blacksmith, turns scrap metal from bombs left from the 1960's and '70's into gardening tools.

These are just a few projects transforming weapons of death into weapons of peace. Embrace life and peace.

One of those with Jesus...drew (his sword), and struck the slave of the high priest, cutting off his ear. Then Jesus said to him, "Put your sword back...for all who take the sword will perish by the sword. (Matthew 26:51-52)

Lord of life, help us to transform violence and death into peace and life.

S H H H H H H !

Even at a low level, constant noise is injurious to health. Constant low-level noise:

- causes kids living with it to release more cortisol, a stress hormone, during sleep
- increases the risk of heart attack
- stifles productivity and motivation
- slows hospitalized patients' healing
- stresses people, increases the chance for mistakes

So, how can you lessen the noise?

- If you must use headphones, be sure only you can hear the music.
- Listen to nature. Take a walk, run or bike without earphones.
- If work is noisy, choose silent sites for lunch; silence at home.
- Skip video games before bedtime.
- Meditate or at least sit quietly.

Silence is healing, calming, energizing. Choose quietness; enter into silence.

> **For everything there is a season, and a time for every matter under heaven...a time to laugh...a time to keep silence, and a time to speak. (Ecclesiastes 3:1,4,7)**

> *Let me choose healing, calming silence over numbing, injurious noise, Jesus.*

A Match Made in Heaven

Tom Packard and Dave Dorlen had failing kidneys and needed new ones if they wanted to survive. Their wives wanted to donate a kidney, but opposing blood types didn't allow it.

Then, independently, Ann Heavner Packard and Roz Dorlen heard about kidney swapping in which a healthy partner gives a "matching" kidney to the sick partner of another couple–and vice versa. The couples were soon notified of a match.

After a series of mental and physical tests and three months of waiting, each woman donated one of their kidneys to the men. At the four surgeries there were 48 surgical personnel. Each was successful and each man received a kidney that saved his life.

After meeting, the couples became fast friends. When Dave Dorlen later needed bladder surgery, the two wives stayed together in the waiting room. The four are also working to increase awareness about live kidney donation.

What can you do to help someone struggling with illness?

**Those who are generous are blessed.
(Proverbs 22:9)**

Inspire those working to find the causes and cures for various diseases, Divine Physician.

K Is for Kitten

It's never too early to encourage children to show compassion for other people – and other creatures. That's what Erin Kennedy's mom did.

She told her soon-to-be 8-year-old daughter that she could either have a birthday party with just a few guests, and she could keep her presents – or she could have a big party with gifts going to a good cause that she could choose.

Erin picked the big celebration with her guests bringing items to support Three Little Kittens, a shelter in Asbury Park, New Jersey, that rescues homeless kittens. The birthday girl received blankets, kitty litter, toys and other items to help the rescued cats from her friends. In turn, the shelter sent each child a "thank-you" photo of a kitten that had been saved.

We can do so much good if we just combine our concern with a spark of the creativity God gave us.

Of every living thing, of all flesh, you shall bring two of every kind into the ark, to keep them alive with you; they shall be male and female. (Genesis 6:19)

Creator of all, thank You for the opportunities You offer us to help sick, abandoned and abused creatures great and small.

Words of Wisdom from E-mails

See tons of junk e-mail? Luckily, mixed in with the silly (or worse) spam are some thought-provoking ones. Here's a recent one.

To realize the value of...

ONE MONTH, ask a mother who gave birth to a premature baby.

ONE WEEK, ask the editor of a weekly newspaper.

ONE HOUR, ask lovers who are waiting to meet.

ONE MINUTE, ask someone who missed the train.

ONE SECOND, ask someone who just avoided an accident.

ONE MILLISECOND, ask someone who won a silver medal in the Olympics.

Remember, yesterday is history. Tomorrow is mystery. Today's a gift. That's why it's called the present. And that's a thought from another e-mail.

Take My instruction instead of silver, and knowledge rather than choice gold; for wisdom is better than jewels, and all that you may desire cannot compare with her.
(Proverbs 8:10-11)

Whet my appetite for wisdom, Holy Spirit.

Quality Lunch

What could be better than enjoying a homemade lunch in the middle of a busy work-day? The answer is enjoying a homemade lunch with the folks with whom you work.

Lisa Marie Rovito of Brooklyn, New York, and about half-a-dozen co-workers decided that instead of always bringing individual brown-bag lunches to work, they would share the home cooked lunch one of them had prepared every Monday.

One man cooked southwestern-style chili; a woman made her boyfriend's Sicilian grandmother's meatballs. A colleague from India prepared slow-cooked lentils and fragrant basmati rice; another woman prepared tasty tacos. A native New Yorker in the group picked up cannoli from a favorite bakery for dessert after homemade chicken and mozzarella heroes.

You never know what may come from shared time over lunches—brown-bagged, homemade or whatever. Enjoy your co-workers' company.

There is nothing better than that all should enjoy their work. (Ecclesiastes 3:22)

May we enjoy the company of others each and every day, Carpenter of Nazareth.

The Priest Who Joined the Circus

Rev. George "Jerry" Hogan's business cards are embossed with a circus tent and a clown. He knows his way around an elephant and rubs elbows with the human cannonball.

This Massachusetts priest is national circus chaplain, a part of the Catholic Church's ministry to people on the move–those who travel with carnivals and sports teams; on the race-car circuit; and migrant workers.

Father Hogan spends half his time at his Boston-area home parish and the rest with the circus. As a youngster, he was a circus buff, but chose the priesthood instead. These days he's getting the best of both worlds–and he hopes that he can be part of the big top for many more years, making sure that faith always finds its way to the center ring.

God's goodness is all around us. We've just got to help others see the details of His presence in our everyday lives.

My eyes have seen your salvation...a light for revelation to the Gentiles and for glory to Your people Israel. (Luke 2:31-32)

Reveal Yourself to me, let me see Your Face, let me know Your presence, Promised of Ages.

Stress: What to Do With It?

A recent survey reports that 50% of Americans worry about stress, knowing that it must be managed. Yet many of us are stumped when it comes to minimizing the impact of stress on our health and well being. Sadly, some people continue habits, such as smoking and overeating that worsen stress in the long run.

Experts recommend guarding against stress through health-promoting practices. For example:

Play card games. Harvard University researchers say that they can help even the most stressed-out among us calm down through a positive, fun form of distraction.

Hug. A brief hug and 10 minutes of handholding with a loved one can curb a rise in blood pressure almost immediately.

Exercise. Researchers say that 60% of stressed people can lower their anxiety through regular yoga classes. Or, take a brisk daily stroll.

Good health is both gift and reward. Cultivate that gift, now.

We have this treasure in clay jars.
(2 Corinthians 4:7)

Teach us to respect and honor our earthly vessels, Lord.

A Modern-Day Hero

Nelson Mandela was born in 1918 in South Africa, the son of a prominent advisor to the king of the Thembu tribe. While studying for his law degree, he joined the African National Congress (ANC) and worked for equal rights for non-whites despite the country's apartheid system.

Mandela was often arrested. In 1962, he was accused of sabotage and plotting to overthrow the government and sentenced to life imprisonment on Robben Island, off Cape Town. He refused to renounce armed struggle for black rights in exchange for his freedom.

Finally, after 27 years imprisonment, Nelson Mandela was freed in 1990, as apartheid was finally ending. At age 75, he was elected president of South Africa in the country's first free elections. He went on to receive the Nobel Peace Prize.

Every one of us has the responsibility to work for justice, whatever the cost.

Blessed are those who hunger and thirst for righteousness. (Matthew 5:6)

Blessed Trinity, You taught us that there is great strength in weakness, great truth in silence. Help us in the struggle for equality for all Your sons and daughters.

A Lesson From The Guy Next Door

Here's a thought-provoking story you may have heard before. After Jack's dad died, he spent extra hours with Harold Belser, a neighbor who taught him carpentry and helped filled the void his father's death had left.

Years later, after Jack grew up and moved away, he received a call that Belser had died. Returning home for the funeral, Jack and his mother visited the man's house one last time. Jack looked for a mysterious small box his neighbor kept on top of his desk that he said contained what "mattered most"–but it was gone.

Two weeks later, Jack came home from work to find a package. Inside was that box, and inside that, a beautiful gold pocket watch with the inscription, "Jack, thanks for your time! Harold Belser"

In all our lives, it's the time we spend loving and caring that makes worthwhile the days we spend living and doing.

Where you go, I will go; where you lodge, I will lodge; your people shall be my people, and your God my God. (Ruth 1:16)

Bless me with the patience to take time to show Your love to those I love and care about, Gentle Savior.

A Lifetime in Four Minutes

Can four minutes change the world? Ask Jason McElwain, the autistic team manager of his Rochester, New York, high school's basketball team. During the season's final game, Coach Jim Johnson put him in with four minutes left.

"I wasn't so much worried about the game," Johnson said. "I was worried that J-Mac might not score."

The crowd's thundering approval rang through the gym until McElwain missed his first shot. Then his second.

It wasn't until his third attempt that he made his first basket. And then another. And then another, until at the end of the four short minutes, he had scored 20 points.

The team, the crowd, even the opposing team, exploded in a deafening cheer for McElwain.

The story of hope and determination touched lives around the world and was honored by ESPN as the "Moment of the Year" in 2006.

The world can change in a matter of minutes. How are you using your time?

Time and chance happen to...all.
(Ecclesiastes 9:11)

Lord, show me how to use each moment to make my world a little bit better.

I Am My Brother's Shaper

Researchers have long studied what shapes us—or, at least, what shapes us most. They've pointed to our parents, particularly our mothers. They've targeted our genes, and our peers.

More and more today, however, scientists are concluding that those who help most to define us are siblings.

If we have brothers and sisters, they are, from the time we are born, our collaborators and conspirators, our role models and cautionary tales. Considering that our spouses arrive later in our lives and that our parents eventually die, siblings may be the only people we'll ever know who truly qualify as partners for life.

"Siblings," says family sociologist Katherine Conger of the University of California, "are with us for the whole journey."

As members of God's human family, we need to see each person as brother or sister—and make sure that our actions affirm and uplift the God-spark in each one.

Do not speak evil against one another, brothers and sisters. (James 4:11)

Father, may I always show Your love and kindness to those around me.

Finding New Meaning

As a young doctor at North Carolina's Duke University, Harold Koenig was ambitious and proud of his strength. He "climbed mountains, swam a mile a day and lifted weights." He also felt "a powerful calling to bring the love of God to the sick. I felt like an energetic vessel for God's healing work."

But things changed when Dr. Koenig was diagnosed with psoriatic inflammatory arthritis. His immune system was attacking his tendons and joints. Any repetitive use could trigger inflammation. It was progressive and incurable.

Dr. Koenig experienced moments of fear and despair. But with the support of loved ones and prayer he found new meaning in life.

In time, Dr. Koenig was able to pray, "Maybe that's what I'm supposed to do, learn to follow God with the pain—and then help others do the same. Lord, that sounds hard. But if you're with me, I'll try."

Honor physicians. ...The Lord created them; for their gift of healing comes from the Most High. (Sirach 38:1-2)

Our plans are not always Yours, Holy Wisdom. Guide me in the path You set before me.

Rebuilding a Community

For eight years, Rhoda Frazier and her family lived very quietly in their Omaha, Nebraska, apartment. "We were always trying to be respectful of our neighbors," she said.

But they wanted a home of their own, so Frazier enlisted the help of Holy Name Housing Corporation. Started in 1982, the nonprofit group builds and renovates homes and sells them to low and moderate income families.

"We were seeing more and more people whose wages were not increasing and yet housing (cost) was drastically increasing," said Sister Marilyn Ross, RSM, executive director of Holy Name Housing Corporation.

They have built or renovated over 500 homes. One of them belongs to the Fraziers. "I love it," says Rhoda Frazier.

The ability to help your community lies within your heart. How can you unlock that gift?

**The fruit of good labors is renowned.
(Wisdom of Solomon 3:15)**

Holy God, I will give to others as You have given to me.

She Loved Baseball

Effa Manley is not a name instantly associated with baseball. But in 2006, this Philadelphia, Pennsylvania, native became the first woman elected to the Baseball Hall of Fame in Cooperstown, New York.

Co-owner and business manager of the Newark Eagles from 1936 to 1948, Manley ran one of the most professional organizations in the Negro Leagues before major league baseball was integrated. A players' advocate, she fought for better schedules, travel and salaries.

She also used her position to crusade for civil rights. In 1934, she organized a boycott of stores in New York's Harlem that refused to hire black salesclerks. A year later, 300 stores there employed blacks. And in 1939, at an Eagles' game she promoted "Anti-Lynching Day."

Manley's gravestone reads, "She loved baseball." That's true. But she loved justice even more.

How will you be remembered?

The compassion of human beings is for their neighbors, but the compassion of the Lord is for every living thing. (Sirach 18:13)

Master, guide my efforts to do Your will today.

The Nose Knows—Really!

"Smell is a potent wizard that transports us across a thousand miles and all the years we have lived." So spoke Helen Keller about our olfactory sense.

Smells can lift our spirits, calm us—and maybe even help us lose weight, according to some. Certain odors are life-savers, like those that spell trouble, such as the smell of smoke or spoiled food.

After years of research, two American scientists decoded this mysterious sense, capturing the Nobel Prize in medicine in 2004 for their efforts. Richard Axel and Linda Buck found the almost 1,000 genes responsible for our ability to recognize and remember some 10,000 different odors—the way we tell the difference between the sweet scent of a hyacinth and the harsh sting of ammonia.

Now that we know how the nose knows, each day we should savor every sniff.

God arranged the members in the body, each one of them, as He chose. ...As it is, there are many members, yet one body.
(1 Corinthians 12:18,20)

With every breath, Dear Lord, I give thanks for Your everlasting mercy.

Make the Most of Mentors

Have you ever wished that, rather than doing everything on your own, you could benefit from the experience of other people who have enjoyed success?

That's exactly what having a mentor can give you. And many men and women of achievement are happy to pass along their wisdom to others who ask them for help. Sheila Murray Bethel, a business speaker and writer, offers these suggestions to help make the most of your relationship with a mentor.

- Look on your mentor as a source of inspiration and information, not a replacement for action.
- Be careful of your mentor's time. Take notes and avoid repeating the same questions.
- If you ask for advice—take it! Don't reinvent the wheel.
- Report back on your actions and the results.

After you've gained from a mentor's guidance, be willing to do the same for others. Pass along your help and knowledge.

A disciple is not above the teacher, but everyone who is fully qualified will be like the teacher. (Luke 6:40)

Generous Creator, show me how to listen and learn from others.

Much Needed Warmth

Nobody wants to think about babies living their first moments gasping for air or being isolated in incubators. But the preemies in the neo-natal intensive care unit at Montefiore Medical Center in the Bronx, New York, are also greeted with smiles and love and not just by their parents.

Elena Melfa, a unit nurse since 1979, noticed that the babies liked to have their feet covered so she knitted blankets for each of them. Little did she know how heartfelt this gesture was.

After one little girl died, her mother thanked Melfa for the blanket. It was the only thing her baby had ever had. "The parents can see you care," says Melfa. "You can see the look of relief."

Next time you're visiting a patient in a hospital, think about all the acts of kindness that touch patients in so many ways. Do your own good deeds for others.

I led them with cords of human kindness, with bands of love. I was to them like those who lift infants to their cheeks. I bent down to them and fed them. (Hosea 11:4)

May our loving actions hug both helpless infants and their parents, Spirit of Life.

A Little Dab of Color

The next time you walk into a church, look at the windows. These are usually not the plain ones that grace homes around the globe. Rather, these windows use the color and imagery of faith to greet people whenever they look at them.

Stained-glass is difficult to work with, but incredibly pleasing to the eye. Debora Coombs, an artist who has worked on windows for St. Mary's Cathedral in Portland, Oregon, for several years, believes that stained-glass is a means to communicate important stories and deepen people's faith–whatever it may be.

"I don't teach faith," says Coombs, "but I can offer something that allows viewers the opportunity to connect."

Study your church's stained-glass windows. You may find a spiritual connection you never thought you had.

Both we and our words are in His hand, as are all understanding and skill in crafts.
(Wisdom of Solomon 7:16)

May art connect us with our faith, Lord of Light.

Honestly Now!

It's sad but true. Not everyone is honest. You need to protect yourself from identity thieves. Writing in *AARP Magazine*, Sid Kirchheimer offers tips to help keep you safe from scams:

- Don't carry many credit cards or a checkbook; lock them up at home.

- Obtain your credit report annually and freeze access to your credit file if your state's laws permit it.

- Buy a shredder and use it regularly for mail, solicitations and other papers with your personal information on it.

- Write checks using Uni-ball gel pens to stymie forgers.

- Return payment stubs when paying bills, but don't write your account numbers on the checks.

Use whatever high-tech and common sense measures are available against thieves. It's responsible to safeguard yourself and your loved ones from fraud. And be sure that you, yourself, behave honestly.

When a strong man...guards his castle, his property is safe. (Luke 11:21)

Guard us from others' dishonesty; help us to always be honest, Just Judge.

The Holy Core

When writer Karen Dahlen was a college student, she took a class in anatomy. On the radio program, *All Things Considered*, she described her unexpected reaction to attending an autopsy.

"I had entered the study of the human body expecting to learn of our concrete physical existence. Instead, I discovered in a more profound way the human body as transitory and fragile, and, by contrast, the soul as enduring," she says.

"This elusive, yet holy core whispers to me of God, of my ability to know and enjoy Him. It compels me to look beneath the surface, to remind myself that, like me, the lady next door who scowls on her way to the mailbox, or the kids who strut down the street, or my atheist friend who enjoys a good conversation, each bear an undying soul and deserve compassion."

Think about the whole person, body and soul, God has given to each of us.

My heart is glad, and my soul rejoices; my body also rests secure. For you do not give me up to Sheol, or let your faithful one see the Pit. (Psalm 16:9-10)

Thank You, Merciful Creator, for sharing Your immortal life with us.

A Child's Best Friend

Charles Duback says that "enlightenment takes place when one lets his innocence emerge and sees nature and life with a childlike awe and respect."

Writer C. S. Lewis, perhaps best known for his thought-provoking and heartwarming *Narnia* series, said that it's in the innocence of a child that one can find the essence of life. He always treated children as his equals and respected them and their viewpoint.

One can see this in *The Chronicles of Narnia* with its struggle between good and evil in worlds populated by talking animals, fantastic beasts and a leonine Christ-figure.

Respect your own inner child. Then you will understand that our world and its creatures are bursting with mystery and wonder–and deserve our best stewardship.

(Jesus) called a child, whom He put among them, and said, "Truly I tell you, unless you change and become like children, you will never enter the kingdom of heaven."
(Matthew 18:2-3)

Open my mind, heart and eyes to see the world of wonder and mystery sprung from Your hands, Father of all.

Moving Out of Yesterday

It can be hard to appreciate today when we cling to yesterday. Here's what happened when one woman let go of the past.

A job change sent Laura DeCando and her husband from New Jersey to Rhode Island. For months, they lived in a hotel, then an apartment before they could move into their house. In the meantime, they spent most weekends returning to New Jersey to visit family and friends.

DeCando says she wasn't happy until she "met a woman who was also a recent transplant. She told me she also had a difficult time adjusting until a friend said to her, 'Concentrate on what you have and not what you don't have'."

DeCando did—and soon realized what a lovely town she and her husband had moved to and started making friends. She eventually became president of the New Neighbors Club.

Make the most of where you are to be who you are.

O give thanks to the Lord, for He is good; for His steadfast love endures forever. Let the redeemed of the Lord say so, those He redeemed from trouble. (Psalm 107:1-3)

Holy Trinity, help me to rejoice in the many blessings You give me each day.

A Journey to Love

When Lawrence Park journeyed to Mexico with teens in his youth ministry program, he wasn't expecting miracles.

"I didn't know what would happen with this group of typical teenagers who seemed preoccupied with the daily distractions of life," he told *Columban Mission* magazine about the trip to provide medical services to the poor.

Any doubts were soon eliminated once the group arrived, and started working side by side with volunteer doctors and dentists.

"I watched these young people engage each individual with care and concern, eager to assist in any way they could," Park recalls. "Their eyes lit up with the realization that they could indeed help improve another person's quality of life, even if it is just one small step at a time."

No matter where we find ourselves, our priority must be to reach out in love.

(She) touched the fringe of His clothes, and... Jesus said, "Someone touched Me; for I noticed that power had gone out from Me."... "Daughter, your faith has made you well; go in peace." (Luke 8:44,46,48)

Surround me with Your love, Compassionate Lord. Heal my wounds of sadness and pain.

While You Live

As the article in *Today's Christian Woman* said, "Life on earth is an adventure. Don't miss it." Here are some suggestions:

- Invest in future joy. Reconnect with people from your past.

- Study a portion of Scripture. Memorize it. Reflect on it. Put it into practice.

- Unplug for a day. Write a letter. Wear a sweater instead of turning up the heat. Use candles instead of electric lights.

- Create a likeness of yourself. Use a pencil, crayons, watercolors or clay to record how you are made in God's image.

- Get to know a few of your future heavenly neighbors. Go to a different church occasionally.

Enjoy yourself. Live your life to the fullest. It's never too late.

Let us make humankind in Our image, according to Our likeness. (Genesis 1:26)

Encourage us to live the life You made us to live, Loving Creator.

Preserving the Land

Montgomery County, Maryland, is only 15 miles outside Washington, D.C., yet residents have worked to preserve farmland and open spaces.

Urban sprawl has been contained. Accomplishing this hasn't been easy, given all the competing interests. Compromises had to be made. Yet, according to Dave Marriott, director of the National Trust for Historic Preservation's rural heritage program, "This is the single most successful program in the nation."

Maintaining open land for future generations is vitally important. Studies have linked access to open land to improved mental health; decreased stress and anxiety; improved physical health. Preserving agricultural land is equally important.

Are you willing to sacrifice to meet your current needs; to anticipate the needs of future generations?

Support your...knowledge with self-control, and self-control with endurance. (2 Peter 1:5,6)

Give success to efforts to establish and preserve open, green spaces, agricultural lands, Harvest Master.

Cruel and Not So Unusual

Despite all of the benefits and efficiencies of a technologically savvy generation, it seems something's getting lost in the rapid transmission of electronic messages: Manners.

Megan Gunder, a New York teen, found this out the hard way, when she opened a text message from a friend that read, "Don't call me anymore." Has the impersonal nature of technology made it easier for young people to dismiss the need for courtesy, consideration and compassion?

According to one study, almost a third of teens admit to saying something in an instant message that they wouldn't have said in person.

Parents can intervene. Remind young people that any message too hurtful to say in person shouldn't be sent. If a teen's text messaging gets out of hand, limit or exclude that feature, or get a phone with parental controls.

Be sure to model good manners yourself.

The Lord honors a father above his children, and He confirms a mother's right over her children. (Sirach 3:2)

Help me find the words to reach and teach teens, Father God.

Opening Eyes with Kindness

The sense of sight is one that most people take for granted. For those who do not have this gift, there are people like Meredith Kollmer.

"Part of being Catholic is service to help people in the community," said Kollmer. Her part has been raising and training Seeing Eye puppies since she was ten years old. The training involves taking the puppies most places she goes, including church, stores, and malls and keeping them under control in those hectic environments.

"The puppies help me become a better person; they teach me patience," she said. The patience has paid off–Kollmer has trained eight Seeing Eye puppies and is doing her part to help those in need.

Kollmer says she does it for "people who don't have everything that I do, to help them live a better life."

How can you help those with special needs?

Jesus laid his hands on his eyes again; and He looked intently and his sight was restored. (Mark 8:25)

How can I do my part to help Your children, Merciful Savior?

Tough Topic, but Important

It can be difficult for loving parents to initiate conversations with their children about such sad realities of life as domestic violence and child abuse.

To help parents, editors at *Family Circle* magazine produced a special report. "Some of our findings about what people would do if they saw someone abusing a child or an elderly person sparked meaningful discussions in my family," writes Susan Ungaro. Here are a few ideas:

Define good discipline and encourage your children to tell you if they have a friend in a violent home.

Emphasize respect and consideration especially between women and men.

Temper your talk because verbal abuse is still abuse.

Stress that family violence is a crime and there are protective laws.

Parents are the best people to teach children about tough issues through their lived example as well as their words.

I have set you an example. (John 13:15)

Inspire parents to treat their children, each other and themselves with deep, sincere respect, Spirit of Counsel.

After Hurricanes Strike

After all the destruction brought by Hurricanes Katrina and Rita, some good emerged. The Catholic Extension Society established a Parish Partnership Program that matches parishes and church groups throughout the country with those devastated by the hurricanes.

Rev. Michael Butler, a North Carolina pastor said, "We saw this opportunity to help as part of our parish stewardship." Donations came in the form of money, supplies, prayers, and time. Although the concrete gifts are helpful, the relationships formed are the most meaningful.

High school teacher Bragg Moore says, "For many years, I have taught my students that the Church is universal, that we are responsible for each other. That all became very real when Katrina hit and people began arriving to help us out. These connections that we've made with new friends will never be forgotten."

John Donne wrote, "No man is an island." Let's remember that's true, too, of women, children, churches, communities and nations.

Bear one another's burdens. (Galatians 6:2)

Just Judge, how can I serve those who still suffer from the effects of catastrophic natural disasters?

Doing The Right Thing

Marie Toussaint, on the housekeeping staff at New York's St. Luke's Hospital, found an envelope stuffed with $100 bills stashed behind a pillow. "The envelope fell on the floor, and I took it outside right away because we had another patient in the room," said Toussaint. "I didn't look in it–I just saw it was big money, and walked outside to give it to the nurse in charge."

The money–$12,450–was put away for safekeeping and eventually claimed.

Toussaint's boss said she's a "very honest and a hardworking lady." She adds that her husband and daughters are reward enough. Too, she told the *New York Daily News*, "I worked really hard to have everything in my life...I don't need money. I've got everything God has given to me."

Would that more of us had Marie Toussaint's attitude! We'd all be better off.

Honesty comes home to those who practice it. (Sirach 27:9)

Remind those with money and power that nothing is more important than honesty and integrity, Jesus Christ. Remind all of us.

Inspired by a Stranger

Peg Fuchs of Canton, Ohio, met a woman who she sewed tote bags and filled them with gifts for the women and children at a local shelter for abused women.

That inspired Fuchs to ask her local shelter if they could use similar bags with goodies and necessities for their clients. Receiving a resounding "Yes!" she sewed fabric remnants she got from relatives in the upholstery business into totes.

Then, in her church's bulletin, she asked for donations of soaps, shampoos, toothpaste and toothbrushes to go in each tote. A child's gift— crayons, a coloring book, or a stuffed animal—was added.

Fuchs says, "The moms and their kids are always so happy to receive these gifts. I'm so grateful that a conversation...with a stranger helped me find a way to help others."

How can you help the needy? Could you inspire one other person to do good deeds?

Be doers of the word, and not merely hearers. (James 1:22)

Help me by deeds more than words to be an inspiration to others, Holy Wisdom.

Gifted Hands

You probably know Albrecht Dürer's elegant drawing *Praying Hands.*

According to an often-quoted modern tale, the impoverished Dürer and one of his brothers wanted to study sculpture in Vienna. Since their family couldn't afford it, they decided that his brother would be a miner; Albrecht, a student. Later, his brother's gnarled, work-worn hands inspired Dürer to create the famous masterpiece.

Truth be told, Albrecht Dürer the Younger was the child of a wealthy Hungarian immigrant goldsmith and his prosperous wife. Dürer the Younger was apprenticed first to his father and then to another artist. *Praying Hands* (1509) is a preliminary study for Jakob Heller's Frankfurt altarpiece of the Assumption and Coronation of the Virgin which, sadly, was burned in 1729.

In fact, *Praying Hands* is truly a tribute to God's gifts of artistic talent and creativity used well by one of His children.

What gifts has God given you with which to praise Him?

There are varieties of gifts...varieties of services... varieties of activities, but it is the same God who activates all of them. (1 Corinthians 12:4,5,6)

Divine Master, help me to know and use my God-given gifts—and to appreciate them.

Finding Your Purpose

When her 10-year-old son started getting into trouble by associating with a rough crowd, Tonya Badillo went into action.

She and her husband Gilberto set up a basketball hoop in their backyard and gave local kids a place to hang out. It became a second home where they could stay for dinner or watch a Friday night movie while eating pizza. The teens thrived in this atmosphere of love, respect and enjoyment.

Badillo also thrived. "I just feel that this is what I was placed here to do," she says. "When I hear of local teens getting into trouble, my heart breaks." This mother of four children faced her own challenges as a teen and appreciates how family love and support can change lives.

Tonya Badillo is doing all she can to strengthen healthy loving families. How can you do the same?

Jesus...said to them, "Let the little children come to Me; do not stop them; for it is to such as these that the kingdom of God belongs." (Mark 10:14)

Child Jesus, remind business to support families through their personnel policies.

Room to Read

When John Wood went backpacking in Asia, he never expected to create a nonprofit organization. But in one Nepalese village he learned that the school library had only 30 books. They were kept locked in a cabinet; never used lest they be damaged.

When Wood reached a local site with Internet access, he e-mailed family, friends and colleagues. Within the month they had donated 3,000 books to Nepal.

Wood didn't stop here, but began Room to Read to build schools and libraries. Within four years the group had opened 1,000 libraries. The plan is to bring literacy to 10 million children in rural Asia by 2010.

What started as one man's vacation turned into hope and education for millions of children.

Go with your instinct to help. You can make a difference.

Give, and it will be given to you...for the measure you give will be the measure you get back. (Luke 6:38)

How can we encourage every form of literacy, Holy Spirit?

It Began with Picking Up Quarters

When Louis Stein was five years old, he and his mother saw some homeless youngsters on the street.

"We need to take these people home," the now 15-year-old recalls telling his mother.

Unable to do that, the boy did what he could. He donated $16 in quarters that he found on the street to a local agency that helped children.

In the decade that followed, Louis has organized charity drives that have brought in thousands of dollars to buy toys and clothes for needy kids. He even spent his high school spring break in New Orleans, helping out after the devastation of Hurricane Katrina.

Unsure what he'll do when he grows up, he knows one thing: "I want to keep doing the fundraising because I am pretty sure there will still be problems."

Each of us is needed to make a difference in our world—one good deed at a time.

Stretch out your hand to the poor. (Sirach 7:32)

Help me do my part today, Jesus, to help someone in need.

Mending Friendships

Growing up across the street from each other in Twin Falls, Idaho, Lisa Fry and Paula Turner never doubted their friendship would last forever. But after Fry married, moved to New York City, and had a baby, her letters to Turner suddenly went unanswered.

Finally, Fry called her faraway once-best friend–and was glad she did. The two talked things out, and in the conversation realized that each was as important to the other as ever.

Friendships can be repaired or reawakened; you just have to take action.

- Take that first step. Make that call, or send that e-mail or letter.
- Apologize when you're wrong, even if you've also been wronged.
- See things from your friend's point of view.
- Accept that friendships change.

The things we treasure most in life, like our friends, often need the most care.

Do not judge, and you will not be judged; do not condemn, and you will not be condemned. Forgive, and you will be forgiven. (Luke 6:37)

Look upon my brokenness, Merciful Father, and heal me with Your unceasing love.

Having the Whole World in Your Hands

Don't think you're a superhero? You could be. The potential to be a champion for our earth is yours. Here are some ideas to unleash the "Eco Hero" in you.

- Instead of using poisonous pesticides to ward off squirrels and other critters munching the tasty plants in your garden, try a heavy dose of cayenne pepper. Wash your hands afterwards; reapply after rain.

- Eat more certified organic foods produced without toxic fertilizers, insecticides and herbicides. Grow some of your own foods.

- Volunteer to clean up and protect a nearby river, lake or wetland. Help preserve nearby wildlife and bird habitats.

- Ask family and friends to help the environment.

We have one earth, custom-made for our needs and delight. Together we can make a difference for our home planet.

The Lord, who created the heavens...formed the earth and made it (He established it; He did not created it a chaos, He formed it to be inhabited!) (Isaiah 45:18)

Blessed God, You made the earth with its diverse forms of life, its beauty, its riches. Help us care for it.

Believing—It's a Good Thing

There's a link between spirituality and a "healthy narcissism" that can actually lead to generosity and goodness.

So say psychologist Paul Wink of Wellesley College and sociologist Michele Dillon of the University of New Hampshire.

Their research took a new look at a 1920s study with data about religion and spirituality—the search for the sacred—that had been ignored. Wink and Dillon discovered that social commitment and concern seemed directly related to traditional religion and spirituality present in people's lives.

"Lots of people are saying Americans are becoming less altruistic and more narcissistic," says Wink, "but our study shows that's not true."

Our faith leads us to do good work. Now there's a lifestyle to follow!

If a brother or sister is naked and lacks daily food, and one of you says to them, "Go in peace; keep warm and eat your fill," and yet you do not supply their bodily needs, what is the good of that? So faith, by itself, if it has no works, is dead. (James 2:15-17)

May my actions this day and all days serve my neighbor while praising You, Divine Creator.

Cheering for Lauren

Like all mothers, Laura Wray worries about her daughter. Especially the day Lauren told her she wanted to try out for cheerleading. Wray's heart pounded. Lauren has Down's syndrome and her mother was afraid of the consequences.

Wray gently tried to tell Lauren that she already did so much. However, the next day she came home with a sheet about uniforms. "I'm already a cheerleader!" she said.

The big game came and Wray anxiously awaited halftime. When the cheerleaders started their routine, Lauren was off on the timing and didn't jump as high as the others, but she had on a huge smile the whole time. Everyone cheered and chanted her name; she even received high fives from the crowd.

Everyone is special in his or her own way. Disability can only limit you if you let it, so focus on your strengths and not your weaknesses–and help others do the same.

My servant Caleb, because he has a different spirit and has followed me wholeheartedly, I will bring into the land into which he went, and his descendants shall possess it.
(Numbers 14:24)

How can I help all people who are challenged in special ways, Holy Spirit?

Love of the Land

It's a sad day when a long-beloved project comes to a halt. But it's an occasion to celebrate when the same project comes back to life.

For the gardens of Mount St. Benedict Monastery in Crookston, Minnesota, a decline in the number of Benedictine Sisters and lack of tender loving care meant that the land produced little. Now, with the aid of 35 neighbors who have become shareholders, the land is again fruitful.

"We haven't seen this for some time," says Sr. Anne Marie Geray. Soon, the group hopes to expand the number of gardeners to at least 50 and plant additional crops called "heirloom varieties."

"When I'm in the gardens I feel like the sisters of the past are right there with me," one group member has said. Surely, the sisters would be proud of the shareholders of the land and its revival.

What good ideas are worth revisiting in your life?

They shall plant vineyards and drink their wine, and they shall make gardens and eat their fruit. (Amos 9:14)

May beloved projects find new life, Creator and Sustainer.

Managing the TV

Television is useful and entertaining in moderation. However, children glued to the TV tend to be overweight, have short attention spans and sleep problems. Here are some suggestions from *Prevention* on limiting their TV time and ours:

- Do not watch TV during meals and until homework is done.

- Ask yourself if TV is replacing reading together or going outdoors or enjoying a board game or coloring, etc.

- Limit TV viewing to inspirational and informational programs or watch DVDs.

- Consider hiding the TV; keep TVs out of bedrooms. What isn't seen will not tempt your children or you.

- Do not use the TV as a babysitter: keep toddlers away from TVs; budget older children's TV time.

It's up to adults to regulate the use of television or other media intelligently. Do so today.

Choose what is right. (Job 34:4)

Spirit of Knowledge, help us use TV and all media and technology wisely.

The Tree That Built a House

When a giant mesquite tree grew dangerously close to the windows of an Episcopal church in San Antonio, Texas, congregation members decided to cut it down. Soon afterwards, a call came from Habitat for Humanity to build a house for a local family.

Ralph Schleicher, a woodworker by hobby, thought about the tree he had just helped chop down. It had measured 34 inches in diameter and nine and a half feet to the first branch.

"Can't build a house with mesquite," Schleicher thought. But he could and did make crosses from it–4,000 crosses, in fact. Selling them at churches, art fairs, gift markets and camps across the state, Schleicher raised the total $40,000 needed to build the Habitat for Humanity house.

Every event in life, every life, is connected. The old teach the young; the young inspire the old; one plants, another harvests.

The one who plants and the one who waters have a common purpose, and each will receive wages according to the labor of each. For we are God's servants, working together.
(1 Corinthians 3:8)

Father, help us to experience Your always-renewing love.

The Fruits of Her Labor

Thanks to the tireless efforts of Ericka Wright, a vacant lot in a Kansas City neighborhood has yielded more than just broken glass and weeds.

Wright's grassroots initiative, the Troostwood Community Garden, helped turn a lost space into a fruitful vegetable garden and a learning center for the neighborhood's children.

When she first noticed the lot, she saw an opportunity to improve the lives of the neighborhood's children, who often experienced crime and racial division.

A true entrepreneur, Wright launched the garden, and involved the children from the start. "I thought if the kids could plant something, see it grow and then harvest it and eat it, it would build in them pride," she says.

What a beautiful vision for positive change!

What opportunities lie before you, on this very day, to make a difference in the lives of the impoverished?

Those who oppress the poor insult their Maker, but those who are kind to the needy honor Him. (Proverbs 14:31)

Remind me that the poor need more than material assistance, Lord. May I give freely of myself, my talents and my attention.

Managing Stress

A complete lack of stress is unhealthy. But so is too much. In order to lessen stress without completely eliminating it, Dr. Dean Ornish, writing in *Newsweek* suggests that you:

- Exercise. Consider including yoga.
- Find intimacy and community. Phone a friend. Eat dinner with your family. Own, walk, and care for a dog. Worship and take part in other events at your church or synagogue.
- Take slow deep breaths.
- Meditate.
- Cut back on caffeine.
- Work at being forgiving, altruistic, compassionate.

Balancing stress—or anything else can be difficult, but it's worth the effort for our well-being.

Seek the Lord...seek righteousness, seek humility. (Zephaniah 2:3)

Divine Physician, give me the wisdom to live the human life You would have me live.

Katrina's Caterer

The night before Hurricane Katrina struck the U.S. Gulf Coast, Bob Ford catered a gospel concert in his native Mississippi. When no one showed up because of the wicked weather, he and his wife Jocelyn took turkey legs and corn on the cob to a shelter in Jackson that was housing 1,200 evacuees.

He, his wife and their two teen daughters returned to that shelter the next day and many more mornings after that. They cooked and served eggs, bacon, sausage, hash browns and grits to crowds as large as 1,700.

Although Ford's own house did not escape Katrina's wrath, that didn't stop him from setting up a wedding feast for a couple who had planned to get married in New Orleans.

"We have to focus on what God wants us to do," said Ford.

What is the Lord calling you to do today?

Morning by morning He wakens—wakens my ear to listen as those who are taught. The Lord God has opened my ear, and I was not rebellious. (Isaiah 50:4-5)

Master, open my ears, help me to make a difference in Your name.

Staying Positive in Tough Times

Kimball Minor, a full time home health aide, had dreamed of buying a new home for her family once she completed college at night. But on August 29th, 2005, her dreams were washed away by Hurricane Katrina. The 31-year-old New Orleans resident lost everything.

Kimball Minor and her children evacuated to Lewisville, Texas, where she found a job as a receptionist at a crisis relief agency.

At a work luncheon that November, Minor got the surprise of her life. An anonymous donor was giving $25,000 to a needy family that had overcome adversity and stayed positive and strong–and the family chosen was hers!

This generous act of kindness is allowing Minor to finish her degree, and keep alive her dream of buying a home for her family.

Prayer, hard work and a positive attitude can overcome adversity–with others' loving support.

Beloved, do not imitate what is evil but imitate what is good. (3 John 11)

Savior, some people use disasters as an excuse for dishonesty and blaming others. Remind us to instead support those hurt by catastrophes with our prayers, our time and our treasure.

Tell Me That Story One More Time

It's a familiar scene: Your elderly grandparent or parent is repeating that story about hardships in the 1930s or what it was like to own a television in the 1950s, and you just can't seem to get interested – again.

Rather than dismiss your loved one's repetition as a symptom of "old age," why not really *listen*?

According to care-giving experts, reminiscing and reviewing stories from the past, especially sad ones, can be quite therapeutic to the elderly. The process of telling and re-telling events and anecdotes can help clear up minor depression, reverses feelings of isolation and helps produce a calming effect. Seen from this angle, perhaps a well-worn story becomes refreshed and new again.

Remain mindful of your elderly loved one's emotional and mental health needs, as well as physical health needs.

Love is patient; love is kind. (1 Corinthians 13:4)

Father, teach me to show love through unending patience.

God's Time

Does God have time for you?

If you've ever felt distant from the God you know to be eternal and all-powerful, you may not perceive His truth–and His love for His children–as well as you might.

"To enter God's time is to accept that He is always available. He's not hiding way off in the future. God is available now," says Philip Yancey, author of *Prayer: Does It Make Any Difference?* "The common question, 'How can God listen to millions of prayers at once?' betrays an inability to think outside time. God's infinite greatness, which we would expect to diminish us, actually makes possible the very closeness we desire. A God unbound by our rules of time has, quite literally, all the time in the world for each of us."

So the more worthwhile question you might ask is: Do I have time for God?

The Lord is good to those who wait for Him, to the soul that seeks Him. It is good that one should wait quietly for the salvation of the Lord. (Lamentations 3:25-26)

Holy Trinity, help me be open to You every moment of my day and my life.

Take This Job – and Love It

"A good job is one of the greatest blessings a person can have," says Nevadan Greg Hoit who drives a concrete mixer. "That's what I want to teach my kids and grandkids." Here are his thoughts about finding work you'll love every day.

Find a job with your name on it. Make sure it's something that you'll be good at and like doing.

Recognize your job's importance. Whatever you do, your job has an impact on people.

Don't stress out. Expect the unexpected, and accept that there will be challenging and disappointing times.

Trust God. See the difficulties of any job as "God moments," times when you turn to God for help and guidance, trusting that His love will never let you down.

The number one job for us all is to reveal God's love to a waiting and needy world.

Go into all the world and proclaim the good news to the whole creation. (Mark 16:15)

This day, and every day, I pray that the work of my hands may give You praise while showing Your love, Spirit of God.

Anonymous Heroes

Who's your hero?

Chances are that you're thinking of someone close to you whom you admire and respect, not someone who's famous.

Daniel Boorstin, historian, author, and Librarian of Congress from 1975 to 1987, wrote, "In our world of big names our true heroes tend to be anonymous. In this life of illusion and quasi-illusion, the person of solid virtues who can be admired for something more substantial than his well-knownness often proves to be the unsung hero: the teacher, the nurse, the mother, the honest cop, the hard worker at lonely, underpaid, unglamorous, unpublicized jobs."

Think about the heroes in your life. They are probably good people who made a difference to you and others by doing good. Think about yourself. If you're trying to do the same, then you, too, just may be somebody's hero.

I have set you an example. (John 13:15)

Show me how to share Your goodness with others, merciful and generous Savior.

Are You Being Honest?

Nobody wants to be called a cheat. Unfortunately, that doesn't mean that people are always honest.

And, from corporate boardrooms to the next cubicle, today's workplace offers far too many examples of lying, stealing and other types of dishonest behavior. And the next generation of workers may not be any better.

The Josephson Institute of Ethics conducted a survey of high school students and found that 61% have cheated on an exam in the last year; 39% have lied to save money; 28% have shoplifted; 23% have stolen from a family member.

Michael Josephson, president of the Institute, asks, "What makes us think these kids won't cheat or steal at work?"

Good question. Parents–and all responsible adults–need to teach youngsters the importance of honesty through both words and deeds.

Live your values and encourage others to do the same.

Honesty comes home to those who practice it. (Sirach 27:9)

Spirit of Counsel, guide me in all my dealings with others. May I always be the honest and honorable person You expect.

Helping after Heartbreak Hotel

When Hurricane Katrina made landfall on the Gulf Coast, it displaced more than 2,800 employees of the Marriott hotel chain.

To help its people, the company hung banners and handed out t-shirts at shelters to advertise a toll-free number workers could call. Marriott gave each affected employee $500 in cash, housed and fed many in hotels, and paid everyone through September. Worldwide, other employees gave up vacation days to keep displaced employees on the payroll beyond that time.

"My dad was a very compassionate man and treated his people very well," explains J. W. Marriott Jr., whose parents, J. Willard and Alice S. Marriott, began the company almost 80 years ago. "The corporate philosophy is: Take good care of the associates, and they'll take care of the customer."

When it comes to big problems, every little bit helps add up to big solutions.

The Lord bless you and keep you; the Lord make His face to shine upon you, and be gracious to you; the Lord lift up His countenance upon you, and give you peace. (Numbers 6:24-26)

Lord, shower all whom I love with Your blessings and peace.

Keeping God in Mind at Work

In *Catholic Digest,* Brian Finnerty listed seven helps to be mindful of God at work.

- Work is important to God, so start by offering your day to Him.
- Say short prayers or brief Scriptural quotes throughout the day.
- Keep a visual reminder of God, say a nature scene or a religious image, in your work area.
- Use the day's difficulties to remind yourself of God and to unite yourself with Him.
- Do the best job you can. Think how Jesus would have acted in the same situation.
- Realize that your work serves others.
- Work hard, but don't be a workaholic. Observe a weekly Sabbath of rest; God and family matter.

Your work can glorify God while it helps you and others. Give it your best.

Commit your work to the Lord. (Proverbs 16:3)

Abide with me, Jesus, Carpenter from Nazareth, as I work and as I keep a weekly Sabbath of rest.

For Good Sportsmanship

Louisiana State University's football team may have been ranked fifth among the nation's collegiate football teams, but some would argue it takes first place for good sportsmanship.

When Hurricane Katrina devastated the Gulf Coast in 2005, the team turned its practice field, located in Baton Rouge 80 miles north of New Orleans, into a rescue and operations center.

The field became a heliport for evacuees; the field house, a patient ward. Other LSU sports followed suit. The basketball arena was turned into a hospital; the band area, a triage center.

Perhaps most poignant is the image of droves of LSU athletes, filling up a tractor-trailer with donated clothes, shoes and other items needed by the storm victims.

The importance of good sportsmanship permeates all areas of life, not simply sports. Every interaction with another is an opportunity to play fair, and put others' needs first.

Jesus...tied a towel around himself. Then He poured water into a basin and began to wash the disciples' feet and to wipe them with the towel that was tied around Him. (John 13:3,4-5)

Inspire those who wrestle with ethical and moral issues, Just Judge.

What a Difference a Word Makes

According to motivational speaker Jim Rohn, there are four words that can make living worthwhile.

Learn: What we don't know *will* hurt us. Learn throughout your lifetime, beyond the classroom. We can learn by paying attention, listening and talking with others.

Try: A natural extension of learning is trying. We learn through attempts to master something. Effort is the materialization of a desire to learn something.

Stay: Sometimes, perseverance and "stick-to-it-iveness" is the best path to success. When the going gets tough, hang in there.

Care: If you care at all, you'll see results from your efforts. If you care enough, you might see incredible results.

How can your life be enriched through this simple approach?

Enjoy yourself. (Ecclesiastes 2:1)

Remind me, Lord, to pray for help in achieving my goals.

Dreams of Space for All

When another little girl told Becca Robison, at the age of ten, she couldn't be an astronaut because it was a "boy's job," she didn't get discouraged.

The Utah native, now a teen, whose love for science began when her older brother taught her about constellations, decided to create a special camp. She called it Astro Tots Science Camp for Little Dippers. Robison held day-long workshops in her own backyard to teach other girls about planets and technology.

When word of the camp spread, Becca Robison was asked to hold camps in local parks and community centers. She even received a special presidential honor for her efforts.

When asked what the science camp had been like, Nicole, one of the campers, said, "Becca teaches you stuff you never knew before and inspires you."

When in doubt, don't give up on your dreams. Your ambitions will inspire others.

Encourage one another. (1 Thessalonians 5:11)

Protect, bless, encourage and inspire all who want to do non-traditional work, Abba.

The Extra Angel

Maggie loved angels. And so, as the school year ended, she shopped for small angel pins to present to her daughter's religious education teacher and to the leader of the parish program. For some reason, she bought three pins instead of two, and decided to keep the third in her pocketbook.

Two weeks after delivering her gifts, Maggie met her friend Carmen. In the course of conversation, Maggie discovered that Carmen had recently been told that her cancer was back–and chemotherapy had to start immediately. In fact, Carmen was on her way to treatment that very afternoon.

Maggie reached into her purse, and found the third angel. There was a reason she had bought it after all.

Stay alert. Watch for opportunities to share your faith and gifts with others; to comfort, console, strengthen and give hope.

Because you have made the Lord your refuge, the Most High your dwelling place...He will command His angels concerning you to guard you. (Psalm 91:9,11)

In my fear and pain, I call to You, my God, praying for Your light and strength.

A Gift of Cows

Going to a wedding? Give a cow. Need to get back in a parent's good graces? Give a cow. Visiting a grieving, sick or needy friend, give a cow.

That's the tradition of the Masai people of Enoosaen, Kenya. And that's what they wanted to do for the people of the United States after the September 11, 2001 attacks.

The elders decided to donate 14 prized bulls and heifers. Elder Mzee ole Yiamboi said "The handkerchief we give to people to wipe their tears with is a cow."

But there was a problem getting the cattle from Kenya to the U.S. So the American ambassador to Kenya announced that instead the cattle will stay in Enoosaen, be blessed, and their offspring used to pay for the education of Enoosaen's children.

The human need to comfort the grieving is universal; its many expressions part of the beautiful mosaic that is humanity. Whom do you know who needs comforting?

A man who had died was...his mother's only son, and she was a widow....(Jesus) had compassion for her. (Luke 7:12,13)

Lord of Life, show me how to comfort those who grieve the loss of loved ones.

Surviving and Striving to Smile

When Tania Head, as one of 122 volunteer guides at Ground Zero, gives a tour, she speaks from experience.

She was in the south tower on the morning that two airplanes struck the World Trade Center on September 11, 2001.

Knocked unconscious by the impact of the second plane, she awoke in searing pain. Burned, bleeding, nearly blinded by dust, she struggled to a stairway, and managed to make her way down 96 floors before the building collapsed.

Her husband, however, was not so lucky; he died in the north tower. Telling her story is Head's way of coping. "If I get sad and cry, then everybody cries," she will tell you. "You have to keep that smile coming."

There are tragedies in every life. Surviving requires a firm focus on the God who is the source of all love and strength.

I, I am He who comforts you; why then are you afraid of a mere mortal who must die? (Isaiah 51:12)

In times of sorrow, trouble and fear, hold me tightly, Lord, in Your everlasting arms. Surround me with love.

From Gangster to Evangelist

John Pridmore was a London gangster. He was known as an enforcer because of his acts of violence. Then, one night in 1991, a voice came to him; he was reminded of all the horrible things he had done.

Pridmore knew he had been given a second chance and decided to change his ways. He now gives lectures in schools, churches, and prisons. He's showing his gratitude to God by helping others.

When journalist Gregg Watts approached Pridmore about writing his biography, (*From Gangland to Promised Land*) Watts found his own life changed. Deciding to be honest with God, Watts even went to confession and left knowing he was "taking the first step on my journey back to my Father."

Everyone can be close to God and encourage others to be the same–gently, respectfully and humbly. Whom have you helped lately?

If you truly amend your ways...act justly...do not oppress the alien, the orphan, and the widow, or shed innocent blood...(or) go after other gods...then I will dwell with you. (Jeremiah 7:5,6,7)

Help us act justly, Abiding Master.

Sisters for Wildlife

When Megan and Mariah Wika visited San Diego's Zoo they enjoyed "an up-close-and-personal look at some of the animals (they) had studied and researched." Already interested in wildlife, the Blaine, Minnesota, sisters decided to do something to "protect endangered species."

First, they saved babysitting money and donated it to the World Wildlife Fund. Then Mariah designed 10 different animal bookmarks. Together, they printed and laminated the bookmarks for sale at school and to family and friends.

Their parents are "thrilled that they've taken such an active interest in conservation issues at a young age."

Megan and Mariah Wika sold $1,000 worth of bookmarks; their parents matched it and the sisters gave the World Wildlife Fund $2,000. Not bad for then 13 and 15 year-olds.

How can you and your children use your talents to protect endangered species?

A man, going on a journey, summoned his slaves and entrusted his property to them. (Matthew 25:14)

May we and our children conserve the earth and all creatures which You have entrusted to our stewardship, Loving Creator.

Baking a Difference

When Michael Gualano saw scenes of the destruction after Hurricane Katrina, he wanted to do something for the affected people. "I felt bad for them," he said.

The nine-year-old from Mamaroneck, New York, got busy—and got baking. A fifth grader who wants to become a chef, he spent two days making brownies, cookies and other treats. His mom helped him with the "oven part" and with cutting. "He wouldn't let me do anything else," she said.

Michael even got his grandmother to make madeleines and a local bakery to donate cupcakes.

And when his five-hour Saturday bake sale ended, he had $387 to send to the American Red Cross.

"I felt happy that I was helping someone," said Michael.

Indeed, the smallest deed, done with great love, can make a big difference for others—and for how we see ourselves.

Truly I tell you, unless you change and become like children, you will never enter the kingdom of heaven. (Matthew 18:3)

Enable us to be generous, Jesus, that we may reach out with love to our sisters and brothers in need.

A Spirit Undefeated

Susan Retik can attest that long-distance power-cycling can invigorate and strengthen more than one's leg muscles.

On September 11, 2001, her husband, David Retik, was killed when American Airlines Flight 11 crashed into New York City's World Trade Center. Retik was overcome with loss, but wanted to do something positive.

She joined with another 9/11 widow, Patti Quigley, who had also lost her husband in that day's terrorist attacks. And, after discovering that they were both fitness buffs, they also realized another common bond: a desire through "a cycling marathon to raise money for Afghan women," says Retik.

Launched in September 2004, Cycling Forward sent $150,000 for food, health education and vocational training to CARE and two other global relief organizations.

These women were able to transform tragedy into a fresh chance for others. How can you transform loss into gain?

Though I walk through the darkest valley, I fear no evil; for You are with me. (Psalm 23:4)

Comfort those who have come face-to-face with loss, Good Shepherd.

Retirement? No, Thank You

How does one go from working as a banker for 33 years to becoming an innovative director of a non-profit food bank? Just ask Don Schinzel.

When he accepted early retirement, he knew he could not just sit around the house. "You can retire, but you can't quit working or you die pretty soon. You have to figure out what to do."

Schinzel did figure it out. For 13 years now, he's built up the Omaha Food Bank from a small non-profit organization to one that includes additional programs, such as offering healthy lunches to school children and giving meals to low-income elderly men and women.

"It's nice to do what you want to do and know you are making a difference," says Don Schinzel. "For me it's living out what Jesus said about taking care of the poor."

What can you do for others?

You gave Me food...something to drink... welcomed Me...gave me clothing...took care of Me...visited Me. ...As you did it to one of the ...members of My family, you did it to Me. (Matthew 25:35,36,40)

May we be able to see You, Merciful Savior, in those who need our compassionate caring.

More Than Just a Can

More than 20 years ago, a simple aluminum can inspired Ruth Hana to do good.

On her way home from work, Hana saw about 40 beer and soda cans on a neighborhood hillside. She gathered the cans and turned them in for the deposit money.

At that point she made an inspired decision. She would organize a community-wide campaign to collect cans and donate proceeds to charity. Her first charity of choice was the Milwaukee County Department of Human Services to help neglected children.

Now a member of the Milwaukee County Senior Citizens Hall of Fame, Hana has helped raise more than $55,000 over the years.

In the right hands, those were more than just humble cans. So, too, with you. How can you do good with something humble?

He spat on the ground and made mud with the saliva and spread the mud on the man's eyes, saying to him, "Go, wash in the pool of Siloam."...(he) came back able to see.
(John 9:6-7)

Inspire our good deeds, Holy Wisdom.

Dealing with Meanness

Too many children from kindergarten through high school experience cruel words and actions from fellow students. These bullies are insecure and take their aggression out on others.

Girls, in particular, form cliques to create an "inner circle" that keeps others out. Their aggression takes a variety of forms: nasty remarks, mean jokes, total ostracism.

In order to cope, a youngster who is being treated badly by classmates needs to remember:

- This isn't your fault. You don't deserve this treatment.
- You aren't alone. Lots of kids go through this.
- Don't suffer in silence. Tell your parents or a teacher.
- Find one friend you can trust.
- Don't retaliate. Meanness turns into more meanness.

Parents need to help their children through difficult situations and not ignore problems, hoping they will go away.

In great and small matters cause no harm. (Sirach 5:15)

Beloved Lord, help me to model kindness and goodness in all my relations with others.

A Word about English

Do you ever find yourself pausing in mid-sentence because you're not sure what's correct—not your facts, but your grammar? Or do you cringe when you hear someone say, "Come to lunch with the boss and I" or "Who forgot their umbrella?"

English is not an easy language. Over the last 1,500 years or so it has not merely evolved from Anglo-Saxon with its Germanic roots, but absorbed large quantities of Latin, French, Italian, Spanish, Greek and more. So our words, as well as our rules, are inconsistent.

"If English weren't so stretchy and unpredictable, we wouldn't have Lewis Carroll, Dr. Seuss, or the Marx Brothers," says Patricia O'Conner, author of *Woe Is I: The Grammarphobe's Guide to Better English in Plain English*. "Life might be easier if we all spoke Latin. But the quirks, the surprises, the ever-changing nature of English—these are the differences between a living language and a dead one."

Enjoy this gift of language—and use it well.

Have a firm grasp of the word. (Titus 1:9)

May my words always be gracious and truthful, Spirit of Wisdom.

The Perception—and Choice—Is Yours

If you had a choice, would you rather win a silver or a bronze Olympic medal? A study of Olympic medal winners might surprise you.

According to writer Kent Crockett, "Most people would assume the silver medal winners would be happier than the bronze medalists since they received a higher honor, but that wasn't the case. The bronze medalists were found to be happier than the silver medalists.

"The former Olympians explained how they felt about their medals. The third-place winners were thrilled just to have won a medal. The silver medalists, on the other hand, felt like losers because they didn't come in first.

"What happens to you is not nearly as important as how you perceive what happens to you."

Your attitude makes such a difference to your life. Remember that keeping a positive yet realistic approach to yourself and your world can work wonders.

A joyful heart is life itself. (Sirach 30:22)

Holy Trinity, illuminate my soul with Your shining goodness and gladness.

It Doesn't Have to Be November

It does not have to be November for people to come together and give thanks for all that they have been blessed with. In ancient Israel, long before Pilgrims set foot on American soil, the word "thanksgiving" was always present in prayers and at mealtime. Food itself was considered a blessing from God.

Beyond food and eating, hospitality was a factor in thanksgiving. People believed visitors should be revered. Though this does not mean inviting danger into your home, the idea of hospitality to visitors is a way of giving thanks for all that one has.

"Sharing is caring" is a common phrase. And how better to give thanks than by sharing and enjoying good times with family and friends!

Do not neglect to show hospitality to strangers, for by doing that some have entertained angels without knowing it. (Hebrews 13:2)

Generous Giver of every good gift, may we recognize our blessings and be thankful everyday.

One Person's Trash...

Have you ever found yourself cleaning out a closet and discovered a perfectly fine item that you just don't want anymore? It's a shame to throw it away. What do you do?

Well, if you're a member of freecycle.org you can offer it to anyone else who wants it and is willing to pick it up. And in return you can browse on the website for things that you can use. And it's all free.

The idea is the brainchild of Deron Beal who worked for a recycling agency in Tucson, Arizona. There he saw many household, electronic, clothing and other items in good condition which could benefit others. More than two million members in 67 countries find the non-profit site useful in providing ways to give and receive.

The next time you have an idea that might help others, try it. It just might succeed.

Help the poor for the Commandment's sake. (Sirach 29:9)

Show me how to seek the welfare of my neighbor as well as myself, Jesus, my Brother.

A Paean to Sidewalks

Sidewalks: Evenly spaced blocks of concrete, bluestone or slate which connect homes, houses of worship, schools, libraries, shops, in sum the whole of a neighborhood or town. They tempt children to explore, discover, find friends.

According to Carolyn Egan of South Windsor, Connecticut, "by chauffeuring (children) everywhere, we also encourage...selfishness and parochialism. Adult maturity is rooted in the unstructured roaming of childhood."

In a *Newsweek* essay, Egan says that for youngsters in the back seat of the car "the destination had displaced the journey." No muscle power, no self-motivated expeditions connect one place and one person with another.

For that matter, try telling these same car-confined children about safety or endurance in extreme temperatures, rain and wind.

Walk and enjoy sidewalks. Encourage your children to use them, too.

Old men and old women shall again sit in the streets of Jerusalem, each with staff in hand ...and the streets of the city shall be full of boys and girls playing. (Zechariah 8:4-5)

Bless children playing on the sidewalks of their cities, towns and villages, Child Jesus.

Cooking With Hope

On September 11, 2001, all 73 employees of the Windows on the World restaurant in the World Trade Center who worked that morning were killed; the restaurant itself obliterated.

Nearly five years later, those not working at the restaurant that day opened Colors, an upscale restaurant in the NoHo area of Manhattan.

The menu includes recipes from Haiti to Thailand, Colombia to Egypt, Italy to China contributed by the diverse staff. Support for the venture came from a nonprofit fund, a foreign cooperative, and even Catholic nuns from California, Michigan and Ohio.

"After 9/11, the only thing that keeps us going is belief in each other," said Fekkak Mamdouh, a Moroccan-born former Windows waiter. "We can't fail."

Whatever the pain in our own lives, God's own hope and joy as well as the support of other people can help us through.

(You) took me from the womb; You kept me safe on my mother's breast. ...Since my mother bore me You have been my God. Do not be far from me, for trouble is near and there is no one to help. (Psalm 22:9,10-11)

Father, bless me with all good things. Fill me with the hope that comes from knowing you.

Stay Healthy

One way to stay healthy is to know the warning signs of illness and ways to avoid unhealthy behaviors. For instance, knowing about strokes and the following prevention tips might help you avoid one.

- **Know Your Numbers**–Philip Gorelick, M.D. says we should know our "blood pressure, cholesterol level, blood sugar level, weight, daily caloric intake, and ...minutes of exercise."

- **Watch Your Diet**–Eat smaller, low salt, low fat portions. Increase salads, vegetables and fruits. Go easy on snacks.

- **Get Active**–Check with your doctor then use low-impact workouts. There are programs for those with physical limitations.

- **Stop Smoking**

- **Get Support**–Family and friends are important.

- **Explore Alternative Medicine**–Yoga, meditation, medical massage and acupuncture are natural ways to relax and heal.

- **Ask Your Doctor**–about the latest treatments and medications.

Take care of your health. (Sirach 18:19)

Creator, teach us how to care for the wonder-filled bodies, minds and souls with which You have gifted us.

One Punk Under God

Jay Bakker, the son of televangelists Jim and Tammy Faye Bakker, has rejected the norm. His arms are covered in tattoos; his head, shaved; a lip, pierced.

After his parents were abandoned by many members of their church during their '80s sex and financial crisis, Baker became "disillusioned with the church...But disillusionment is good, because then you don't have any illusions."

Bakker joined the Revolution Church, a ministry aimed at disaffected young people who feel unwelcome in more conventional congregations.

Each of us seeks God in our own way. Let's strive to love and respect our neighbors in their journeys—whether or not we believe the same things.

Do not judge, so that you may not be judged. For with the judgement you make you will be judged, and the measure you give will be the measure you get. Why do you see the speck in your neighbor's eye, but do not notice the log in your own eye? (Matthew 7:1-3)

Good Shepherd, You accept and love me. Help me to treat others in the same way.

Caring for a Natural Cause

Although global warming is in a worldwide spotlight, many are not changing their habits. The truth is that the smallest actions can make a resounding change in our environment.

Junk mail, which most people throw out, is a huge waste of paper. Ask to be removed from companies' mailing lists. You'll save trees and water; the annoyance, too.

Replace one roll of virgin-fiber toilet paper with one made from recycled paper. If every U.S. house did this, 424,000 trees would be saved annually. Ditto for paper napkins for a saving of one million trees annually.

Fact: the net cooling effect of **one** healthy tree is equivalent to ten room-size air conditioners operating 20 hours a day!

Remember, too, to reuse, recycle and/or donate computers, cell phones, other electronics; rechargeable batteries; printer ink cartridges; household items; clothing.

We have one planet that is our home. Treat it with love.

God took the man and put him the garden of Eden to till it and keep it. (Genesis 2:15)

Lord of all, remind us to cherish the Earth which You have given us.

Don't Fear Imperfection

Most of us want to do the best we can. Sometimes we get hung up on trying to be perfect. That's a shame because struggling to reach an impossible goal can keep us from achieving everything we're really capable of doing.

Writing in *The Spirituality of Imperfection,* Ernest Kurtz says, "A spirituality of imperfection suggests that spirituality's first step involves seeing one's self as one is: mixed up, paradoxical, incomplete and imperfect. Flawedness is the first fact about human beings. And paradoxically, in that imperfect foundation, we find not despair but joy. For it is only within the reality of our imperfection that we can find the peace and serenity we crave."

This doesn't mean that we don't try to improve ourselves or our world. It means that since we're both sinners and beloved children of God, we need to trust Him to help us bring out the best in ourselves.

Cast all your anxiety of Him. (1 Peter 5:7)

Beloved God, help me strive to be my best self for love of You.

Asking the Right Question

Rev. William Maestri, of the Catholic Archdiocese of New Orleans, told *Our Sunday Visitor* that it's a mystery why God allows bad things to happen to good people.

The better question, Rev. Maestri said is, "What do good people do when bad things happen?" According to the Bible, he said, we must refuse to be bitter, make a deeper commitment to our neighbor and trust in God's grace to get us through.

The discussion concerned how people coped in the aftermath of Hurricanes Katrina and Rita, but the advice can apply to anyone overwhelmed by catastrophe.

Mary Wimberly, both a recovery worker and one of those who suffered personal loss from the storms, acknowledged the enormity of the disaster. But, she said, "We fully trust that when Christ taught us to pray 'Give us this day our daily bread' that He meant it."

Especially when it's hard, keep the faith.

Father, hallowed be Your name. Your kingdom come. Give us each day our daily bread. And forgive us our sins, for we ourselves forgive everyone indebted to us. (Luke 11:2-4)

Holy Spirit, I do trust. Increase my trust.

Pennies from Heaven?

Teacher Niki Rockwell wanted her students at the Groton-Dunstable Middle School in Massachusetts to grasp the enormity of the Holocaust. "How will they understand 1.5 million children, 6 million Jews?" she asked.

So they launched the penny project: a drive to collect a penny for each child killed during the Holocaust. Families, neighbors and local businesses supported the effort and after months of work they had 267,000 pennies.

Then Rockwell realized that some of the containers had been stolen. Rather than give up, the students redoubled their efforts. Word got out and people, many of them strangers, arrived at the school, pennies in hand. Some came from a biker on a Harley-Davidson. Some came from a survivor of a concentration camp. Within days the students had reached their goal. And they've decided to make the pennies part of a permanent memorial to the children of the Holocaust.

Good can come from a bad situation, if we make the effort.

Each builder must choose with care.
(1 Corinthians 3:10)

Loving Creator, remind us how connected we are to each other, to the past and to the future.

Always New Things to Learn

Scientists know how and why leaves turn from green to bright yellow and orange in the autumn; but not why they turn red.

Science writer Corey Binns says that leaves stop producing green-tinted chlorophyll when temperatures are chilly and daylight limited. "The orange and yellow pigments called carotenoids... shine through the leaves' washed-out green."

But red comes from "anthocyanins, which are only produced in fall." Red pigments, as seen in northern maples and ash trees, block harmful solar radiation, protect cells from freezing and are antioxidants. But if leaves turn red too early that's also a sign of distress.

"Scientists hope (that) studying anthocyanins will clue them into the degree to which some trees are stressed, which could provide a better picture of environmental problems early on," says Binns.

Throughout your life remain curious and interested about everything, especially Nature. There's always something to learn.

The trees of the Lord are watered abundantly...in them the birds build their nests. (Psalm 104:16,17)

Keep us curious about the lovely world You created and which You sustain, Father of all.

Time Out Corner, Please

Nobody wants stress, and yet everybody has it. Though there's no fool-proof method of avoiding stress, there are ways to ease its damaging effects:

- Daily Exercise: Allison Whaite knew her health was in trouble when she ran away from stress by over-eating. Now, she runs away from stress by literally running, keeping her heart and head healthy.

- Therapy: A 2004 study on 1,500 women concluded that there is a correlation between a need for anger management therapy and heart disease. It's not only emotionally healthy to talk, but physically helpful as well.

- Support Network: When Mary Farley, a heart-attack survivor, realized stress was literally killing her, she rounded up friends: "Friends provide a whole different kind of support."

Again, there's no single way to erase stress, but there are many ways to ease and manage it.

Be quick to listen, slow to speak, slow to anger; for your anger does not produce God's righteousness. (James 1:19)

May we find laughter, love, and hugs when we need them most, Holy Redeemer.

Lending a Helping Paw

Notre Dame-Bishop Gibbons School in Schenectady has a new student–a young yellow Labrador Retriever named Molly. Science teacher Ralph Provenza rescued her from an animal shelter, and she is now being trained as a pet therapist to help in nursing homes, hospitals, and other facilities.

Seven students are helping to train Molly. They play with her, and take her on walks. It's hard work, but also something they enjoy. In addition, the students are writing an English/Spanish training manual and producing a video illustrating Molly's training.

These students' task is important because the training Molly receives will benefit more people in the future. You see, this special dog will eventually help people who need special assistance. Molly will lend a helpful paw so others can continue living as normally as possible.

Enjoy the animals in your life. Treat them well.

Receive her in the Lord...give her any help she may need from you, for she has been a great help to many people. (Romans 16:2).

Thank You for enabling the handicapped to more fully participate in life with the help of service dogs, Blessed Trinity.

Thanks and Praise

Even before Francis of Assisi had sung his famous *Canticle of the Creatures* in the winter of 1224-25 in Italy, the Iroquois of the northeastern U. S. and Canada had composed their own thanksgiving hymn to God, the Great Spirit. Here are excerpts:

"We return thanks to our mother, the earth, which sustains us...to the rivers and streams, which supply us with water...to all herbs which furnish medicines...to the moon and stars, which have given to us their light...to the sun, that has looked upon the earth with a beneficent eye.

"Lastly, we return thanks to the Great Spirit, in Whom is embodied all goodness, and Who directs all things for the good of Her children."

Do we, like the Iroquois and like Francis of Assisi, sing–and live–our gratitude to God for his good gifts, his tender care for each of us?

The Lord created human beings out of earth, and makes them return to it again. ...He established with them an eternal covenant, and revealed to them His decrees. (Sirach 17:1,12)

Creator and Sustainer, may my deeds and words be my thanksgiving hymn to You for everything You have given and continue to give me.

A Voice of Greatness

"Maybe you will have a lot of joy with this growing child," a doctor told a woman who had just given birth to a "Thalidomide baby." She thought he was crazy.

But her child, Thomas Quasthoff, now in his late 40s, is an internationally respected and award-winning German opera and *lieder* singer. He stands 4'4" with a stunted stature, missing arms and flipper-like hands caused by the drug which was given to his mother to relieve morning sickness.

His condition did not stop Quasthoff from pursuing his dreams of learning music, teaching and singing. Nor has it prevented him from marrying and enjoying his life.

"I don't think I have to prove to me or to others that I am able to do it," he says.

Live life to the fullest—and encourage others to do the same.

Do not speak evil against one another. (James 4:11)

Savior, may all of us, especially those with special challenges, accomplish our dreams, no matter what others may think.

Things Lost and Found

"We've all lost something prized and irreplaceable and we've all felt bereft and at the same time furious at our carelessness," notes Bette Jane Raphael. Because the lost item "meant something to us, and that made it a part of us, losing it was like losing a piece of who we are."

Raphael was distraught when she lost a photo of herself, aged four, smiling up at her Dad. She searched frantically, but came to accept that it was gone. Eventually she realized she didn't need the picture to feel love for her father.

Here are tips for coping with loss and regret:

- don't beat yourself up over the loss
- share your feelings and seek support
- consider the loss as an opportunity
- learn to let go of the past
- cherish your memories

Loss is not easy. Mourning is healthy. Healing will come.

Blessed be the God and Father of our Lord Jesus Christ, the Father of mercies and the God of all consolation, who consoles us in all our affliction. (2 Corinthians 1:3-4)

May we console the sorrowing even as You console us in our sorrow, Merciful God.

The Friends around Us

Sometimes we have no idea just how important we are to other people.

Ron Willingham, author of *Integrity Service* tells the story of a bank teller who had formed a casual friendship with an elderly woman who came to the bank once a month. It wasn't until the teller told the woman that she could save time by using the new "drive-through" window that the customer revealed that she had no close family or friends, lived some distance from town, and really looked forward to their chats. More than that, she actually considered the bank teller a good friend.

This changed the teller's attitude about her work. She realized that even the smallest contact with her customers gave her the opportunity to add real meaning to their lives and her own.

Appreciate the value of your relationships. Let the light of God's love shine through your words and actions.

Owe no one anything, except to love one another. ...Love does no wrong to a neighbor. (Romans 13:8,10)

Loving Lord, reveal to me the many ways I can serve You by serving Your people, my neighbors.

Holding Hands—and Holding On

Maryknoll Sisters Theresa Baldini and Madeline McHugh have lost count of the bombings they've experienced as missionaries in the Sudan, Africa. But they do remember the time when 24 bombs dropped around them.

Those among the more than 50 students from St. Bakhita Girls School who couldn't fit into the two bomb shelters, as well as the two missionaries, lay stomach down on the dirt. A young girl, aged 8 or 9, crawled between the two women. Other youngsters were around them, weeping. The Sisters encouraged them to hold hands and pray.

Sister Theresa says that the "bombing made us realize the importance of encouraging those around us to support each other" and that "we are all members of one sacred family."

If we believe that each person, of every race, age, social class, ethnicity and religion are "all members of one sacred family," then we need to seek peace with justice.

The effect of righteousness will be peace... quietness and trust forever. (Isaiah 32:17)

Prince of Peace, show us how to work for peace with justice.

Apples of Love and Life

At age 11, Herman Rosenblat was sent to a Nazi concentration camp with his brothers. One day a little girl threw him an apple over the fence. For six months, the two children met everyday at the same place and she would throw him chunks of bread or an apple.

One day Rosenblat told her that he was being moved and she should not return to that spot again. That was the last time he saw her. He didn't know her name, but he thought of her as his angel.

Years later in New York, he went on a blind date. His date was that little girl–his angel–who had thrown him apples. He proposed to her then and there and they've been together ever since–married for 50 years, with children and grandchildren.

Life takes us on strange paths, but God always sends His angels to help us.

"Was it not three men that we threw bound into the fire?" They answered (King Nebuchadnezzar), "True, O king." He replied, "But I see four men unbound walking in the middle of the fire, and they are not hurt; and the fourth has the appearance of a god." (Daniel 3:24-25)

Lord of Sinai, send Your angels to help Your people.

PB 'n' J—and Love Notes

At the end of a long day, Catherine Madera sat down at her kitchen table and started looking through some drawings her seven-year-old daughter Haley had left there. Other family members were shown doing things with Haley. But the drawing of Catherine showed her on the computer alone.

Feeling sad, the mother of two prayed to connect with her younger child. Later that evening, as she made Haley's lunch for the next day, a blank napkin became the answer.

Using a marker, Madera drew two stick figures holding hands, and wrote the words, "Mommy loves Haley." She then placed the napkin into her child's lunchbox.

The next night the napkin was still inside the lunchbox, carefully folded at the bottom. "I put a note in with Haley's lunch every day after that," Madera recalls.

In the craziness of every day, we need to remember what matters most—loving one another, deeply, sincerely, unreservedly.

**Love one another deeply from the heart.
(1 Peter 1:22)**

Divine Master, help me be present to the people who love me, and whom I love, today and every day.

Writing Wrongs

At some point, each one of us will have a "buying" experience go bad. Although only five percent of Americans complain to store managers or corporate headquarters, there are ways to commit your complaint to paper and make it work for you.

Start your letter with a little sweet talk. Maybe you've been satisfied in the past–and this was a shocking departure from previously good experiences.

Use more effective "snail" mail to send your letter of complaint, not e-mail.

Keep it simple and short. Get to the point.

Apply a little pressure, but no name-calling.

Ask for–and expect to receive–something, for example, a discount coupon, but not necessarily a replacement.

Remember, in such letters as in life, it's best to stand up for yourself–but without stepping on someone else.

Stand firm...be courageous.
(1 Corinthians 16:13)

Guide me on right paths, Paraclete, so I may serve You with my whole being.

Walking to America

Legson Kayira had resigned himself to living in poverty in his native Malawi. Then he read about Abraham Lincoln.

The determination of this American president gave Kayira a goal—go to the United States and get an education. At 16, he set out, on foot, to do that—repeating on the journey words he learned in his village school, "I will try."

On his way, he stopped in Uganda, where he read about a school in Washington State. He wrote to them and eventually they wrote back—sending him money for a plane ticket and offering him a scholarship and housing. The money came from the school and local residents who were inspired by Kayira's story.

Just two years after he had set out from his African village, Kayira had made it to the United States—and had begun to fulfill his dream for a better life.

What steps have you taken to make your dreams a reality?

Bear fruit with patient endurance. (Luke 8:15)

In the darkness, I seek Your light, Savior. Show me Your hope-paved path.

In Pursuit of Justice

A bishop recently asked members of one parish in his diocese if Spanish-language Masses should be offered. Some people objected, saying that immigrants should learn English.

Obviously, concerns about immigration and population present many difficult legal issues and ethical problems. Clear-thinking and mutual respect are essential on all sides—and a broader view of history can help.

Just as we learn about the important English settlements of Jamestown, Virginia, in 1607, and Plymouth, Massachusetts, in 1620, we might recall Spanish settlements of note. These include St. Augustine, Florida, the oldest city in the United States, founded in 1565, and Santa Fe, New Mexico, capital of the province of Nuevo Mexico in New Spain established in 1607.

Today's Americans are descended from those who walked across the Bering land bridge, canoed down the Pacific coast of the Americas or sailed from a European, African or Asian port.

Promote justice, mercy and peace.

You shall not oppress a resident alien. (Exodus 23:9)

Abba, thank You for the skills, artistry and culture of our ancestors and today's immigrants.

Help in Disguise

John van Hengel received the call early one morning. The man on the line said he was coming to make a donation—and van Hengel hoped it would be enough to keep the struggling St. Mary's Food Bank around to serve the poor of Phoenix.

Then he saw his would-be benefactor. Wearing threadbare clothes, the old man stepped out of a beat-up car. Van Hengel, tried to hide his disappointment as he went through the motions of showing him around and telling of the good work accomplished at St. Mary's.

When the man had driven away, van Hengel turned over the check the man had left face down on the desk—it was for $10,000. St. Mary's stayed open. Last year, it distributed more than 25 million pounds of food.

Help often comes to us from the most unlikely of places and people. We just need to be open to God's ever-mysterious ways.

The good person out of the good treasure of the heart produces good...for it is out of the abundance of the heart that the mouth speaks. (Luke 6:45)

Help me, Lord, to see the world as You see it.

Skydiving and Selling Fruitcake

When her daughter died after a long struggle with cancer, Hilda Pearson, 90, decided to do something that might help others avoid similar loss. Included in her plan—skydiving and a raffle.

Pearson was so impressed by the care her daughter, Irene, had received in the oncology unit at Grafton General Hospital in Warwick, Australia, that she organized a fundraiser for it.

For her part, the nonagenarian planned to jump out of an airplane, with the parachute company donating the cost of the experience to the cause. A relative made a delicious fruitcake—the raffle prize—topped with icing that included a butterfly image, a symbol of "new life." Almost $2,000 was raised.

In all that happens, especially difficult times, we need to search for the hope manifested in God's love for us through others.

Jesus rebuked the demon, and it came out of him, and the boy was cured instantly. (Matthew 17:18)

In my hopelessness, Father, show me the light of Your love.

It's Up to Y O U

Ardath Rodale, chairwoman of the board of Rodale, Inc., wrote in *Prevention Magazine*, "Our environment must be treated with the utmost care. Each of us can give back to our beautiful Mother Earth." How?

- Volunteer for organized neighborhood trash cleanups.

- Encourage family, friends and neighbors by your example of ecologically aware living and voting.

- Teach children to value the Earth; to be responsible for its health through their actions and, in time, votes.

- Recycle or compost everything you can–paper, newspapers, cans, glass, aluminum, scrap metal, kitchen scraps.

- Be part of the solution. Use canvas, not plastic, bags, at the supermarket; a programmable thermostat; a clothes line for drying the laundry.

These are just a few suggestions. Remember the earth you leave to your children and theirs is the earth you cultivate today.

The Lord looked upon the earth, and filled it with His good things. (Sirach 16:29)

Creator, remind us to use our intelligence and judgment for the good of Your earth, its creatures and ourselves; and to Your glory.

Putting Her Heart in Their Home

For Niki Sideris, the sight of a Greek woman alone and afraid, unable to speak English, sitting with her sick child in a tiny room has kept her volunteering for 35 years at the Ronald McDonald House in New York City.

Sideris convinced that woman to go to the House established for the families of children receiving treatment for cancer. Sideris has raised $2.6 million in 20 years for the House.

In 1986 she began a Greek division of the Ronald McDonald House. And she raises monies from the Greek community in the U.S. and from donors in Greece.

Widowed 18 months after her marriage, Sideris never had children of her own, but she explains, "I dedicated myself to mothering the sick children of the world."

Reaching out with loving concern can help strangers feel at home. Welcome the stranger, the immigrant, the sick, the elderly and children.

The woman was a Gentile, of Syrophoenician origin. She begged (Jesus) to cast the demon out of her daughter. ...She...found the child lying on the bed, and the demon gone. (Mark 7:26,30)

Redeemer, remind us that You bring healing and help to all children.

A Beast Fable–"Not My Business"

Once upon a time…Mouse found a mousetrap in a farmhouse kitchen and told the other creatures of his discovery.

Chicken said it was "of no consequence" to her. Pig promised Mouse his prayers. Cow said "It's no skin off my nose."

That night the farm wife was bitten by a poisonous snake caught in the mouse trap. She came down with a fever. Chicken soup's good for a fever, so the farmer took his hatchet to the main ingredient.

Then friends and neighbors came to sit with the farmer and his sick wife, so the farmer killed Pig to feed them.

Eventually, the woman died. It was Cow's turn to face the farmer's hatchet–to feed all those who came to his wife's funeral.

The tale concludes "when one of us is threatened, we are all at risk. …We must keep an eye out for one another and make an extra effort to encourage one another."

If I, your Lord and Teacher, have washed your feet, you also ought to wash one another's feet. (John 13:14)

Remind us, Christ, that we are each others' keepers.

Seeing Clearly

It's a real lift for me," said Ohio ophthalmologist Bill Brinker. "I have a skill that meets a need. I enjoy this much more than I would spending my vacation sitting on a beach."

Brinker volunteers with Eye Care International, a non-denominational ministry of Methodists, Lutherans, Church of God, Evangelical Free Church, Jews, Catholics, Southern Baptists, and Presbyterians that he, his wife and friends began almost two decades ago.

According to an article in *Episcopal Life*, Eye Care volunteers go to El Salvador for two weeks. During one stint, over 4,000 patients—farmers, laborers, domestics, students and pensioners—were tested and received reading glasses, prescription eyeglasses, cataract surgery, and even a prosthetic eye.

Volunteer Tom Cliffel says he has "to give back for all the blessings I've received."

How, in your unique way, can you "give back for all the blessings" you've received?

What shall I return to the Lord for all His bounty to me? (Psalm 116:12)

Help me make my life a hymn of thanksgiving, Generous Giver of every good gift.

The Power of Prayer

There may be more to having faith than previously given credit. Recent studies have shown that faith can actually affect one's health—in a positive way, of course.

In 2005, Amy L. Ai, an associate professor of psychology in the University of Washington's health sciences department tested 453 collegians about different stressful situations. These situations included the September 11th attacks, Hurricane Katrina, and open heart surgery.

The study found that a "linkage of spiritual support and positive attitude mediated the effect of...distress."

In short, faith expressed in prayer eases the pains of stress. For many, this is simply another good reason to turn to prayer when the going gets tough.

Pray without ceasing. (1 Thessalonians 5:17)

Merciful Savior, may we find comfort and courage through prayer.

Scoring One for Friendship

Abbas Suan was used to the taunts. While playing for Bnei Sakhnin, a soccer team named for the Galilean town in Israel that had long been his family's home, he'd heard the boos, jeers and shouts of "terrorist" from opposing fans.

Suan is one of just two Arab Israelis on the otherwise Jewish team. When Tomer Eliyahu, a Jew, joined the team in 2003, the two became friends. Like others on the team, they heeded their coach's mantra: "We aren't Jews and Arabs here; we are family."

In 2005, Suan helped his team win game after game. In fact, the team fell just short of participating in the World Cup competition. And the chants turned from, "no Arabs, no terror," to "no Arabs, no goal."

Hearts and minds can change. Through the knowledge and respect which comes via friendships it's possible to overcome learned fear and hatred of those who are different.

Zion shall be redeemed by justice. (Isaiah 1:27)

Give me wisdom and understanding, Gracious Lord, that I may build peace.

To Me, Love from Me

Cheryl Richardson, author of *Take Time for Your Life,* believes that "the best presents are the ones we give ourselves." Consider these gift ideas:

- The Gift of Time. Once a week do an activity just for you—yoga or a massage; meditation, writing in a journal, spending time with a friend; a special time with your children.

- The Gift of Reflection. Think about all the things you have. Do a "thank you" walk around your home. Reconnect with someone. Offer a blessing of thanks before every meal.

- The Gift of Laughter. Take a chuckle break—with a humorous book or a funny movie. Spend time with a friend who always leaves you in stitches.

- The Gift of Kindness. Start the day smiling. Compliment a stranger. Hold doors. Contribute to a friend's favorite charity. Each day, remember that there's one special gift that keeps on giving—God's own great love for each of us.

'To love Him with all the heart, and with all the understanding, and with all the strength,' and 'to love one's neighbor as oneself'—this is much more important than all whole burnt offerings and sacrifices. (Mark 12:32,33)

Remind me, Jesus, that love of my neighbors is rooted in love for myself, as is, warts and all.

God's Second Phone Call

With help from the Mission Doctors Association of Los Angeles, Dr. Richard and Loretta Stoughton and their five children had already served five years as Catholic medical missionaries in Zimbabwe early in their marriage.

But when they were planning to retire, some 30 years later, they heard the "call" to mission again, in a talk by Green Bay, Wisconsin, Bishop Robert Morneau.

Leaving children and grandchildren, the Stoughtons returned to Zimbabwe in 2002. There Dr. Stoughton labors to make a faith-filled difference for those with HIV/AIDS and other ailments at St. Theresa's Hospital. Meanwhile, Loretta Stoughton reaches out to families through Mothers' Prayer Groups.

"We both feel that this is exactly where God wants us to be," says Dr. Richard Stoughton. His wife adds, "Everyone receives a call from God in some way. We must trust in His providence for each of us."

Like good stewards of the manifold grace of God, serve one another with whatever gift each of you has received. (1 Peter 4:10)

Master, may my actions reveal Your love.

"Friend-ing" the Loneliness

Fact: A lot of people are lonely.

Overwhelmed by the responsibilities of work and family, many of us put friendship on the back burner. It becomes a luxury rather than an essential part of a healthy life.

So to fight the loneliness, find friends—and be a friend to others.

Among the keys to successful adult friendships are joining groups that allow you to meet new people. Then, in a friendship, you need to pay attention to the details of a friend's life, remember birthdays, be present for sad and joyful times, and get creative about getting together. Friendships take work—frequent telephone calls or e-mails—and patience; new friendships may take some time to build. Above all, when there's a problem, talk it out.

The bottom line: Make friendship a priority today and every day. After all, the end to loneliness is just one friend away.

A friend loves at all times. (Proverbs 17:17)

In those around me, may I find and share Your goodness, Loving Lord.

600 Pounds of Baby Food

It started with a story Joyce Griste read about Crossroads Urban Center in Salt Lake City, Utah. There, poor people are provided with discounted supplemental food and other basic items.

Griste, along with other women in St. Ambrose parish, organized a drive for baby food and other infant items, such as diapers, baby wipes, lotions, bibs, pacifiers and bottles.

The bins set up in the back of the church filled up fast. In the end, more than 600 pounds of baby food were collected in addition to more than 4,000 diapers, in various sizes, and the other things on the list. Griste plans to make the drive a regular parish event.

Lending a hand to someone in need is one way to see–and serve–Jesus in those around us.

Truly I tell you, just as you did it to one of the least of these who are members of my family, you did it to Me. (Matthew 25:40)

Jesus, help me to see You, Your loveliness, in the faces of my needy sisters and brothers.

With Cell Phones, Silence Is Golden

It's a fair guess that almost all of us have, in some way or another, encountered some form of rudeness involving cell phones. So here are some ways to avoid disturbing or offending others when using that phone:

1. Turn your phone off in restaurants (how must your table companions feel if you ignore them to "yak, yak, yak" on your cell phone?), museums and, especially, movie theaters and in live-theatre performances. If you must remain accessible, activate the "vibrate" feature instead.

2. Be discreet. If you must hold a conversation, go to a private area or outdoors.

3. Be polite. Don't say anything on a cell phone or in a text message that you would not normally say to a person face-to-face.

Cell phones can offer limitless convenience as well as safety. Just don't let them become an impediment to good manners.

Do not be reckless in your speech. (Sirach 4:29)

Holy Trinity, remind me that my words and actions define my character.

Want to Be Healthy in the Future?

Did you ever think that positive emotions, such as feeling hopeful about the future, being happy and enjoying life could improve your heath?

In a seven year study of 1,558 older Mexican-Americans living in five Southwestern states, researchers at the University of Texas Medical Center in Galveston found that "those who scored high in positive emotions were significantly less likely to become frail than those who did not. In fact, as the participants' positive emotions score increased, their risk of frailty decreased."

Researchers think that "positive emotions may directly affect health via chemical and neural responses...(and) by increasing intellectual, physical, psychological, and social resources."

Cultivate hopefulness and happiness. Do all in your power to enjoy life–however *you* define "enjoy." Life and good health are God-given gifts.

There is nothing better for (mortals) than to be happy and enjoy themselves as long as they live. (Ecclesiastes 3:12)

Holy Spirit, help me be hopeful and happy and to enjoy life.

Remembering a Gentleman Giant

When John Mara stood in New York City's St. Patrick's Cathedral October 28, 2005, to eulogize his father, Wellington Mara, the church was filled with heroes from the world of professional football.

But to John and his ten siblings, the real hero was their father as "dad," not as owner of the New York Giants.

"Many years ago his good friend said to me, 'You realize, don't you, that your father is the best example of how we should all live our lives,'" John said. "Over the years, I have come to realize what a role model he really was."

While the elder Mara attended every Giants football game, he found it equally important to be at the First Communion, graduation, school play, and little league game of every child or grandchild. "He was always positive, always supportive, setting yet another example for all of us," John said.

Professional accomplishments in life are praiseworthy. What's more important, however, is how we love while we live.

You love all things that exist, and detest none of the things that You have made. ...You spare all things, for they are Yours, O Lord, You who love the living. (Wisdom of Solomon 11:24,26)

Enable us to be lovers, Lord and Lover of all.

The Power of a Good Steward

If you visit St. Elizabeth's parish in Wyandotte, Michigan, the first thing you'll notice is the windmill on top of the rectory. Unless, that is, you spy the solar panels and solar water heating system above the garage.

Rev. Charles Morris, the pastor, has worked to decrease the church's energy use and carbon dioxide emissions, lowering annual energy costs by $20,000 and reducing peak energy demand by 60% over the last five years. As the executive director of Michigan Interfaith Power and Light, he encourages all denominations to be good stewards of the earth.

"We're all part of God's creation," says Rev. Morris. "If someone like me doesn't speak about its care, who will? The changes we've made here, that's a form of preaching."

Who will, indeed? Each of us has an obligation to protect our home with all its resources and wonders.

As servants of Christ...it is required of stewards that they be found trustworthy.
(1 Corinthians 4:1-2)

Almighty God and Father, inspire us to care for Your great gift to us, Your beautiful planet earth, our home.

Dog Gives Lessons in Compassion

Kim Heater wanted to get her children a dog that would teach them lessons in compassion and charity. So the family went to Greyhound Adoption of Ohio, where many greyhounds once caged and forced to race awaited homes.

They immediately fell in love with Paige and brought her home. Soon, they adopted another greyhound, Jay, because Paige clearly liked him so much.

Adopting the dogs was only the first lesson the pets provided. Heater's youngest daughter told people how important it was to give homes to animals who would otherwise be euthanized because they could no longer race.

Greyhounds are great blood donors, so the Heater family brings their dogs once a month to donate blood for sick dogs.

Paige and Jay have shown the Heater children how important it is to be compassionate.

As God's chosen ones, holy and beloved, clothe yourselves with compassion. (Colossians 3:12)

May compassion be our rule of life, God of Life.

Witness to God's Love

If you say "Salem, Massachusetts" to someone, they will probably reply, "Oh, that's where the witch trials were held."

That's true. In 1692, nineteen people were hanged based on allegations of witchcraft. The real evil: hysteria and bias. Interest in this sad history has led to a thriving tourist business.

Wanting to offer locals and visitors positive spiritual inspiration, the parishioners of Immaculate Conception Church decided to do something. Along with the help of a national organization called Project Moses they erected a stone monument on the church lawn. On one side are the Ten Commandments and on the other, the Beatitudes.

Parishioner Joanne Wright said, "The world has so many illusions. This is a strong statement of God as the Truth and the Rock."

Proclaim God's compassion and mercy for *all* His daughters and sons of every faith and no particular faith.

My heart recoils within Me; My compassion grows warm and tender...for I am God and no mortal, the Holy One in your midst. (Hosea 11:8-9)

Spirit of Counsel, guide our thoughts and deeds so that Your wisdom and love may shine through our words and deeds.

Seeking Greatness

Remember the saying, "You can't see the forest for the trees"? Many people live that way.

That could mean getting caught up in your work rather than considering how much meaning it really has for you. It could mean being more concerned about having a beautiful house than a loving home.

Henry Van Dyke, a clergyman and an educator, is perhaps best known for his book, *The Other Wise Man*. He wrote: "It is only by thinking about great and good things that we come to love them. It is only by loving them that we come to long for them. It is only by longing for them that we are impelled to seek after them; and it is only by seeking after them that they become ours."

Rediscover the forest. Spend some time today thinking about great things. Then do something about them.

In kinship with Wisdom there is immortality... pure delight...unfailing wealth...understanding and renown. (Wisdom of Solomon 8:17,18)

Eternal Father, open my mind to You and the wonders of Your plans for Your people. Help me strive to achieve all the good I can for my sake and for that of my brothers and sisters.

Day of the Dead: A Celebration of Life

Despite its name, the Day of the Dead (Dia del Muerte), is not sad.

Widely celebrated in Mexico, the holiday marks a joyous time of remembrance of loved ones who have died. Observance often includes bountiful meals, parades and placing photographs of deceased loved ones near a long-burning candle, to symbolize the life of their memory in the hearts of the living.

"It's a wonderful, colorful and warm holiday," says one observer. Another says that the holiday serves as a time of honoring his mother, who also observed the celebration. "She would always put up a photo and a candle, no matter how busy she was," he says.

What rituals help link you to your ancestors? How can you honor the memory of those who helped shape who you are today?

He took up a collection...to provide for a sin offering. In doing this (Judas Maccabeus)... (took) account of the resurrection....that those who had fallen would rise again.
(2 Maccabees 12:43,44)

I am grateful for the bravery, perseverance and faith of those who have lived before me, Holy God.

Words to Guide a Century of Living

Mundo wigo, "the Creator is good," were among the very first words her Mohegan Pequot elders taught Gladys Tantaquidgeon.

"The Creator is good" had special significance to her throughout her long life. Born in 1899, Tantaquidgeon came to maturity as age-old Indian wisdom was being obliterated by changing times. In fact, the Connecticut government said the Mohegan Pequots were extinct.

Tantaquidgeon learned tribal history and legends; magic and medicine. She was only the third Mohegan medicine woman since European colonization. A student of history, ethnography and Indian crafts, she became an expert on Mohegan art. With her brother and their father, she began a museum. Gladys Tantaquidgeon lived to see the Pequot Mohegan tribe recognized by the U.S. government in 1994.

Mundo wigo, the Creator is good. Injustices are being remedied. Indian wisdom is being recognized. Recognize wisdom in others and in yourself.

God created humankind in His image, in the image of God He created them; male and female He created them. (Genesis 1:27)

Great Father, help me seek wisdom, justice and peace.

Who Knows What's Right?

Do you get the feeling that many people think that if someone disagrees with them they are not only wrong, but unworthy of respect? We're entitled to our beliefs, but it's presumptuous to think that we have a pipeline to the truth and somebody on "the other side" doesn't.

Here's a thought worth considering: "It is my earnest desire to know the will of Providence. And if I can learn what it is, I will do it.

"These are not, however, the days of miracles, and I suppose it will be granted that I am not to expect a direct revelation. I must study the plain, physical facts of the case, ascertain what is possible, and learn what appears to be wise and right. The subject is difficult, and good people do not agree."

The words belong to Abraham Lincoln. But his point is valid for all of us.

Make me to know Your ways, O Lord; teach me Your paths. Lead me in Your truth, and teach me. (Psalm 25:4-5)

Guide us, Spirit of Wisdom, in seeking Your will. May we always respect the right of others to disagree with us.

Holy Hip-Hop! It's a Rapping Priest!

With Rev. Stan Fortuna, the whole notion of "typical" goes right out the door.

The Yonkers, New York, native is one of the founding members of the Franciscan Friars of the Renewal. In his gray tunic and sandals, and signature gray hat, he ministers to the poor of the south Bronx, New York, using music—from hip-hop to jazz to rap—to convey the Gospel message.

A former jazz musician, Father Stan believes that this way of making Jesus known allows the Gospel to transform lives. "This music affords a whole other way of talking to a whole sector of society," he explains.

Each one of us is called to bring God's light and peace to the world through our lives and work. How we do that is as varied as the songs we sing.

Is not this the Carpenter, the son of Mary and brother of James and Joses and Judas and Simon, and are not His sisters here with us? (Mark 6:3)

Jesus, You spread the Father's good news as a carpenter and through Your life in the family of Joseph and Mary. Help us to do the same in our work and in our families.

Let Go and Let God

When Ann Richard's son, Kingston, declared that he wanted to speak in front of their church's congregation at a program honoring Martin Luther King, Jr., she felt dread, rather than excitement.

Richard knows that in a similar situation, most parents would be thrilled. But all she could think about was that her son, who has been diagnosed with autism, a neurological disorder, would suffer people's derision up on the podium.

Richard admits that her first thought was, "There's no way he can do this."

Through her prayers, however, Richard felt God's presence, saying "Ann, where are you placing your trust?"

In the end, every word Kingston practiced came out crisp and clear. He even got the entire congregation to say the Lord's prayer with him.

Miracles happen every day. It's our job to make sure we don't miss them.

The human mind plans the way, but the Lord directs the steps. (Proverbs 16:9)

Thank You, Abba, for Your involvement in my life.

A Card for a Tip

Edith Simpson's story about tipping motel and hotel housekeepers is unusual and demonstrates the importance of making a person feel special.

While Simpson and her husband were vacationing in Nashville a few years ago they left a tip as always. "But it just doesn't seem like enough," she thought. "I really should leave a bit of encouragement too."

When Simpson returned home she decided to cut the front off old colorful greeting cards that she had received to create new ones with her own messages, often poems or prayers.

She says, "Now, wherever my travels take me, I leave one of these cards each morning on the motel pillow along with the tip...I often get back sweet notes."

Treat everyone not only with justice, but with empathy.

Does not a word surpass a good gift? Both are to be found in a gracious person. (Sirach 18:17)

Jesus, remind me to be gracious in my interactions with other people; grateful, too, for their service and labors.

C'mon Kids—Let's Get Happy!

Young people today are bombarded with schoolwork, afterschool activities, part-time jobs, parental demands, and peer pressures. They're overstimulated by technology and media access. Parents are equally stressed.

In all this "busy-ness," where is the joy? There are ways to create and improve family together-time and increase overall happiness. Some suggestions:

- Before bedtime, sit with your children and talk.
- Take back your day by eliminating one activity to make room for family time. Have family movie or fun nights, but whatever the event, make it a regular practice.
- Plan one-on-one "dates" with your children every week or two.

At all times and at all ages, the best we can do is to just be with and for one another.

Just as I have loved you, you also should love one another. (John 13:34)

Blessed Trinity, You know that it's not always easy or convenient to just be there for one another. Enable us to find the love to do it, no matter what.

The Ticking of a Stop Watch

On November 9, 2006, the world of journalism lost one of its most valued members, Ed Bradley. For a quarter of a century, "I'm Ed Bradley," sounded from television sets across the country to the ticking of the stop watch of the Sunday night news program *60 Minutes.*

Behind the public image of an extraordinary newsman, however, was a man who had inspirational words for anyone in or out of his field.

Ron Allen, a fellow journalist who was close to Ed Bradley wondered how he had achieved so much professionally and earned such an enviable reputation. "So, how the heck did you do it?" he asked. The answer Ed Bradley gave was simple: "Hard work. You've got to really believe you can get where you want to go."

No matter what one is aiming for in life, hard work and perseverance pay off.

You need endurance, so that when you have done the will of God, you may receive what was promised. (Hebrews 10:36)

May we learn from the example of those who have gone before us to be all we can be, Holy Wisdom.

Show Them...They Want to Learn

"Why does daddy yell at mommy?" is one of the questions that some children must ponder everyday. Domestic violence clearly has an impact on children who experience it.

It's important that in a family each member should respect everyone else. Writing in *Family Circle*, Susan Ungaro stresses that parents also need to discuss domestic violence with their children. She explains that parents should define good discipline, emphasize respect and stress that abuse is a crime. Ungaro also says that "96 percent of people believe verbal abuse can do as much harm as physical abuse."

Children need to grow up knowing, not only that they must respect others, but also that they deserve to receive respect. Be a good role model for the young people in your life.

Love is patient...kind...not envious or boastful or arrogant or rude...is not irritable or resentful; it does not rejoice in wrongdoing, but rejoices in the truth. (1 Corinthians 13:4-6)

Protect children, women and men from those who would abuse them physically, psychologically, spiritually or sexually, Savior of those who take refuge in You.

Forging New Connections

"Fear is not something you talk about, but it's there all the time," says Vietnam vet Walter Wills regarding war.

His first-hand experience of fear prompted him to write to today's soldiers. Wills is part of a pen pal program called My Soldier, which gives thousands of veterans and other civilians a way to unite with the new generation of soldiers.

"The highlight of the week was when the mail came in. It was such a big deal to get anything," says Wills. "It was from back home, from the world. And we were out of the world."

"It's a simple gesture intended to show the soldiers that people are thinking about them and are anxious for them to come home safely," Wills added.

Even the smallest acts can make a huge difference. Do all you can to help those in the armed services.

Pray for...peace...within your walls, and security within your towers. (Psalm 122:6,7)

Merciful Lord, how can we care for those serving in the military, their family members and veterans while working for a just and lasting peace?

Ecological Suggestions for Any Holiday

Want to contribute to a charity for the holidays? Here are a few suggestions to accrue money and remind yourself about environmental concerns at the same time. You'll need a jar or bowl:

- No programmable thermostat? Put in 50 cents.
- Add 50 cents for each string of holiday lights.
- Bought gifts that need batteries? Add $1 per gift.
- Daytime thermostat set above 68F? Contribute another $1.
- Don't lower the thermostat at night? Add another $1.
- Don't recycle? Donate $5.
- Add two cents for each light bulb in your home.
- Tire pressure not checked before driving to a family celebration? That'll be 50 cents.

These and other ideas will make you more conscious of the cost of depleting earth's limited resources. Too, you will have collected money to donate to a good cause.

The Lord has made all things, and to the godly He has given wisdom. (Sirach 43:33)

Help us, Creator, to repair Your earth, our home, which we have damaged.

Now There's An Idea!

Inventor. Industrialist. Entrepreneur. Genius. When it came to generating ideas, Thomas Alva Edison was prolific.

But this holder of more than 1,000 patents also had good business sense and vision. He didn't just invent things as an exercise; he became involved in "the long, laborious trouble of working them out and producing apparatus which is commercial."

Edison didn't invent electric light, but he did create the first practical incandescent light bulb. That also meant that Edison had to invent the electrical industry from the ground up: from the concept of a central power station, to the development of safety devices, to the manufacture of switches, sockets and fuses.

While few people have as many bright ideas as Thomas Alva Edison, there is a spark of creativity in everyone. Appreciate, nurture and express your creativity.

To each is given the manifestation of the Spirit...knowledge...faith...healing...working of miracles...prophecy...discernment of spirits... tongues. (1 Corinthians 12:7,8,9,10)

Alert me, Holy Wisdom, to my unique creativity. Then help me appreciate, nurture and express it.

God Has a Reason for It

A woman had leukemia. Her suffering was clearly visible to her distraught children. Her youngest son could no longer bear to see her in such a state and he prayed to God to take her away to heaven and end her suffering.

The next morning, she woke up looking better and was able to converse with her family. Laughter and joy filled the air. That night, the whole family slept in peace. The following day, however, the woman passed away.

It might be difficult to reason why she died just when there seemed to be some hope and why God had not taken her away when she had suffered. The answer may be simple...He may have given her and her family one last happy day together, so that their final memories of her would be ones they could cherish.

God does indeed work in mysterious ways.

God did not make death, and He does not delight in the death of the living. For He created all things so that they might exist. (Wisdom of Solomon 1:13-14)

Christ Jesus, guide the dying through death's door into eternal felicity.

An Honest Lie?

Every day, we have to make decisions. Some are difficult to make, some easy. One of those decisions is choosing to tell the truth or not. As children, we were taught not to lie, no matter what. Yet as we grow older, we realize that in certain situations, brutal frankness may not be the best thing.

Keep consequences in mind. Ask yourself if you are trying to protect the other person—or yourself. Is it important for him or her to know the truth and is it beneficial for the relationship in the long run? And remember that it's important to draw the line between discretion and secrecy.

Honesty is the best policy, though few people are completely honest all the time. What we can do, however, is to be true to ourselves and God and to always strive to be people of integrity.

Honesty comes home to those who practice it. (Sirach 27:9)

Remind all of us, especially those with positions of authority that honesty is the foundation of trust, Just Judge.

Get More out of Sunday Worship

How can Sunday Mass or worship services be more meaningful? Consider these ideas.

Prepare ahead of time. Go over the week's readings beforehand. Think about the Sacred Scripture and its impact on your life.

Sit in a different spot. A new pew might bring a whole new perspective.

Pray and sing with enthusiasm.

See Jesus in the sign of peace. When you greet someone, remember you're offering peace to Jesus Himself.

Leave Sunday worship with a mission. What is God asking you to do to be more Christ-like in the coming week?

Catholic Masses end with the words, "Go in peace to love and serve the Lord." Protestant worship services end by invoking God's blessing on the congregants for the upcoming week. It's because we are blessed and asked to love and serve God in ourselves and in others during the upcoming week that we need to get the most out of Sunday worship.

Give my greetings to...Nympha and the church in her house. (Colossians 4:15)

Each week help me to worship You, God, in Spirit and in truth as well as in deeds.

Like Snowflakes on Your Tongue

Ann had simply had it! Work was insane, overwhelming. There didn't seem to be any time to clean her house—let alone spend the time she so desperately wanted to spend with her husband and her eight-year-old daughter Hannah.

Then one Monday, she took a break from working at home to pick up Hannah at school. As she walked the few blocks from her house to the school, snow started falling. She saw the youngsters leaving school catching snowflakes on their tongues. Soon Hannah was with her—and following the other kids' lead. Then Ann herself joined in.

In those moments that afternoon, Ann's stress and cares melted away as quickly as the snowflakes on her tongue.

Sometimes in life we've got to stop to smell the roses—or play in the snow.

Whenever the evil spirit...came upon Saul, David took the lyre and played it...and Saul would be relieved and feel better, and the evil spirit would depart. (1 Samuel 16:23)

Help me to make time for You and for the self You made me to be, Creator of all that is seen and unseen.

Geography—a Must Know

Many young Americans are geographically illiterate. A survey shows that they don't know where many countries are located on a map.

A specialist in geography education, David Rutherford says, "Young Americans just don't seem to have much interest in the world outside of the U.S." Three-quarters of students, ages 18-24 failed to locate Indonesia on a map even after many of the images shown on television after the 2004 tsunami. "Fifty-four percent were unaware that Sudan is country in Africa (and)…fewer than three in ten think it's necessary to know where countries in the news are located."

The executive director of the Association of American Geographers, Douglas Richardson says, "Knowledge is essential for survival in our rapidly globalizing world. We need to catch up in offering the foundation for students in geography."

It's important that we help the leaders of tomorrow get the knowledge they need today.

Do not forget my teaching. (Proverbs 3:1)

Encourage and support teachers, Holy Spirit. Help them educate Your children for the present and the future.

A Place for Hope

In the 1940s, Seabrook Farms was more than a small New Jersey industrial community. Instead, it was a place for renewed hope for roughly 2,500 Japanese Americans who arrived there after enduring seclusion and isolation at internment camps in the West.

Despite its rigors and distance from their past lives, many of those who worked at the vegetable packaging and processing plant for 12 hours a day regarded Seabrook as a way to renew their hope and to start over.

While Seabrook's facilities were bare bones, families could remain together. Margaret Yoshida, who was 18 when she came to the New Jersey factory town, says that "it was the freedom we had at Seabrook" that made the greatest impression on the Japanese-Americans.

Sometimes, our perception of life's challenges makes all the difference. What we regard as minimal, might seem bountiful in other circumstances. Let's always keep hope in our hearts.

As you did it to...members of My family, you did it to Me. (Matthew 25:40)

Show us how to be people of hope, Redeemer, and to seek justice for all in our nation, our world.

The Love of a Stranger

Ask yourself "What's the most I would do for a stranger?" A charitable act might pop into your mind or offering money to somebody in need. But would you ever spend time with a stranger who simply needed company? A man once did that, with genuine and selfless love.

When a marine was told his father was dying, he went to see him and was taken to a room in the hospital. Sitting there, he took the dying man's hand and comforted him with loving words until the moment he died.

Only later did the marine tell the nurse that there had been a mistake, the old man was not his father. But he had stayed simply because the man was dying and the younger man felt that somebody should be with him as he breathed his last.

The love of a stranger may be hard to understand, but it certainly isn't hard to cherish.

If we love one another, God lives in us, and His love is perfected in us. (1 John 4:12)

Merciful Savior, see to it that no one dies alone, unloved.

When You Wish...

Maybe it's because of life's many harsh realities that humankind has long wished for good luck.

We have hoped for a "lucky break" from wishbones from the time of the Etruscans in 300 B.C. up to our own Thanksgiving feasts. People have also wished on the first star they see in the evening for over two thousand years.

According to a folklore expert, the custom of throwing coins into wishing wells got started in medieval Europe. People thought the spirits that dwelled there would answer their prayers.

Today, we still toss coins – and they may help others' wishes come true: workers at Walt Disney World, for instance, regularly fish out the pennies from the park's wishing wells and donate the thousands of dollars to children's charities.

We can't always have our heart's desires, but we can always trust God to hear us when we tell Him about them.

I have put my hope in the Everlasting. (Baruch 4:22)

Keep us hopeful in Your salvation, Divine Master.

Listening and Caring

When was the last time you heard an elderly relative speak about his or her past? Were you annoyed? Delighted? Curious?

For elderly people talking about their past "helps clear up minor depression, reverses feelings of isolation, and helps...boost physical and mental well-being" according to an article in *Spirituality and Health Magazine*.

Next time you visit an elderly relative:

- Look for an object—a book, knickknack, clothing, for example—to spark a conversation.
- Use scents because they bring back memories, even if your elderly relative cannot verbalize it.
- Make "reminiscing cards" using pictures from magazines or newspapers showing scenes from the past.
- Listen to unhappy memories; let the elderly person express sadness and doubts.

Kindness will never be forgotten.

**Kindness is like a garden of blessings.
(Sirach 40:17)**

It isn't always easy to be patient with relatives, Holy Spirit. Help me.

A Different Thanksgiving

On the fourth Thursday of November, most Americans celebrate Thanksgiving by being with their family; eating too much; and watching football games on TV.

But some families are more creative. Writing in *Christianity Today* Susan Kildow says that after their feast her family goes bowling to unwind, laugh and compete.

One Thanksgiving morning Amanda Cody took a hike with her boyfriend and his family. They shared funny stories and listened to music during the car ride; then hiked and savored Creation's beauty.

Kate Bryant asked each family member to write down something God had done for them the previous year. Then they read their notes aloud and said together after each: "Give thanks to the Lord, for He is good, His love endures forever."

Gratitude to God is paramount at holidays and always.

Do not forget all His benefits—who forgives... who heals...who redeems...who crowns you with steadfast love and mercy, who satisfies you with good. (Psalm 103:2-3,4-5)

Thank You, God, for all You give us today and everyday.

Make More of the Holidays

From Thanksgiving through Christmas and finally New Year's Day, the holiday season offers wonderful opportunities to develop spirituality and help others.

Jeanne Winters, author of *Inspirational Home*, offers ideas:

- Write a journal listing all the blessings and reasons to give thanks that you and your family have had this year.
- Ask a local shelter what its clients need. Have family, friends or co-workers provide the items and then make Christmas gift boxes or baskets at a party before delivering the presents.
- At the end of the year, make time to engage in earnest reflection and to forgive anyone towards whom you harbor resentment.

Try not to let the rush of the holidays interfere with the joy that can be found in our daily lives, if we would only look for it.

If you seek Me with all your heart, I will let you find Me, says the Lord. (Jeremiah 29:13-14)

Jesus, our Messiah, remind us to make room for You in the busyness of our day-to-day tasks. And remind us, too, to reach out to others in need of Your loving kindness.

Finding God by Candlelight

With three young children and busy jobs, Brendan and Kate struggled to keep spirituality a part of their family life–until one November evening, when the lights went out during a storm.

The family of five sat around a lighted candle in their living room, telling stories and laughing together.

That was the start of this family's "candle night," a once a week event when they would sit around a flickering flame and tell stories–family stories, saint stories and Gospel stories.

In the moments of darkness of our every day, it's good to remember that the light and hope of Christ is ever-present to light our way.

For you who revere My Name the sun of righteousness shall rise, with healing in its wings. (Malachi 4:2)

Light up our darkness, Promised One, with Your light. Help us brighten the lives of all Your people we meet day by day.

The Golden Rule Gives Back

Richard Kubach, owner of the Melrose Diner in Philadelphia, uses the Golden Rule for his employees as well as customers: *Do unto others as you would have them do unto you.*

Unfortunately, this didn't always mean a lot of profits. That's why Kubach depended on the day before Thanksgiving, one of the busiest, most important days of the year for any restaurant. That's also why it was such a crisis when a water main broke and flooded the diner's basement.

"There was so much water and mud in the basement. Thanksgiving would come and go with the restaurant's doors closed," believed Kubach.

But when word spread, employees, customers and neighbors pitched in. Nobody wanted to see the Melrose Diner go under. Within hours, the diner had been brought back to life.

"Do unto others as you would have them do unto you" is always a good policy.

The commandments...are summed up in this word, "Love your neighbor as yourself." (Romans 13:9)

Merciful God, please remind me that while respecting others as You respect me is often neither easy nor practical, it is always right.

Why the Pilgrims Still Matter to America

It's easy to overlook some facts about the Pilgrims, the first European colonists in what's now the state of Massachusetts.

"The Pilgrims were America's first illegal immigrants. Their patent did not apply that far north," says Nathaniel Philbrick, author of *Mayflower*, in *Yankee* magazine. They were originally headed toward the mouth of the Hudson River, but landed at Plymouth because of unfavorable weather and winds.

The Pilgrims were unprepared for the bitter New England winter. But the Patuxet and Massachuset Indians taught them how to grow food, especially corn; harvest wild food and hunt game. "Here are two very different groups of people–English and Indian–yet for 50 years they made it work," continues Philbrick.

"It wasn't easy; they didn't necessarily understand each other or like each other, but they worked at it because the alternative was a war that could destroy everything. ...The world is a lot like that now."

Let's continue to work for harmony.

The Lord lifts up those who are bowed down... watches over the strangers. (Psalm 146:8)

Unite our nation of immigrants, Gracious God, under a government of, by, and for the people.

Happy Holidays, Minus the Debt

From Thanksgiving through Christmas and beyond typical expenses often include traveling to visit family and friends. "Throw in the expense of multiple gifts, elaborate meals and endless rolls of shiny, pretty paper" and it all adds up according to an article in *Real Simple*. The magazine addressed this problem with tips from readers on ways to keep costs in check:

- Avoid last-minute shopping; buy items year round and catch the sales
- Don't run up credit-card debt; pay in cash.
- Give homemade gifts, for instance, fudge, salsa, or pesto.
- Keep things in perspective: time with your loved ones is the greatest, most precious if least expensive gift of all.

For the happiest of holidays, make time for the things that really matter.

Just as I have loved you, you also should love one another. (John 13:34)

Remind us, Jesus, that to give the gift of our presence, attention, concern, interest and love to one another is to give the best gift of all.

Writing Off Persistence

Joan Medlicott sent her manuscripts–about women in their 60s–to one publishing house after the other. The response was always the same. "They all said, 'Thank you, it's beautifully written, but nobody cares about older people'," recalls Nancy Coffey, Medlicott's agent.

But the two kept at it, determined to find someone to publish the works. Their persistence eventually paid off. Today *The Ladies of Covington* is a popular series and the forerunner of a new genre tentatively called "matron lit," exploring the concerns and contributions made by women in what one author describes as "second adulthood."

"I knew nothing about novel writing," says Medlicott. "I took classes, hired an editor, read copiously and kept on going."

Reaching a goal often requires hard work and a healthy dose of commitment. But, in the end, what we accomplish can sometimes make our lives–and the lives of others–that much better.

The glory of youths is their strength, but the beauty of the aged is their gray hair. (Proverbs 20:29)

Bless me with Your wisdom, Master. Guide me in Your ways.

Connecting with the Reason for the Season

The core meaning of Christmas is easy for most to understand. Simply put, it's a celebration of Jesus' birth.

Yet, fewer among us understand the significance and beauty of Advent, Christmas' predecessor.

Too often lost in the flurry of activity between Thanksgiving and Christmas, Advent is intended to be a beautiful interlude, a time to pause reflectively, to think, to pray and to prepare for Jesus' coming into our hearts and for His coming in glory.

An Advent wreath can serve as a perfect reminder that what we are awaiting is not just Christmas, but Christ Himself. Too, the wreath can be seen as a symbol of each year with Christ at its center.

Make Advent a happy time of prayer and expectation.

The Son of Man is to come with His angels in the glory of His Father, and then He will repay everyone for what has been done. (Matthew 16:27)

Come again in glory, Savior Jesus!

Justice in the Face of Injustice

What constitutes justice? For Rosa Parks, it was positive action against what was then legal, but clearly unjust.

On December 1, 1955, Parks, an African-American seamstress, boarded a bus in Montgomery, Alabama, paid her fare and sat down. Three stops later, a white man boarded, paid the fare, but had to stand. Bus driver James Blake told Parks and three other black people to get up. She refused: "No. I'm tired of being treated like a second-class citizen."

She was arrested, fingerprinted and photographed and four days later fined $10 plus $4 court costs. Then Rev. Dr. Martin Luther King, Jr. led a 381 day boycott of the city bus system which helped change the laws.

An informed and active citizenry is vital to democracy. When was the last time you read the Declaration of Independence, U. S. Constitution, or the U. S. Bill of Rights?

The Lord has anointed me...to proclaim liberty. (Isaiah 61:1)

Remind me, God, that because governments derive their "just powers from the consent of the governed" I have an obligation to be an informed and active citizen.

Advice from the Rabbi

Parents struggling to find family time, relax! The Rabbi's in the house! The author of 16 books on parenting as well as host of the television program, *Shalom in the Home,* Rabbi Shmuley Boteach offers this advice to moms and dads.

Talk. That's a parent's main tool.

Turn off the television. When the family's gathered for dinner together, have a conversation.

Limit time with friends. Family gives children something that no one else can.

Skip some of the extracurriculars. Stop pushing for straight As. Give hugs and kisses. Many people are successful mostly because of the love they had in their lives.

Choose family over work. The need for professional satisfaction is fine, but work should never be the first priority.

While you're trying these tips, give thanks for being part of a family—and pray for those who don't have one.

Honor your father, and do not forget the birth pangs of your mother. (Sirach 7:27)

Jesus, who grew to adulthood in the home of Joseph and Mary, inspire parents as they work to strengthen their families.

Thinking beyond Borders

Organizing a consistent daily routine is often impossible when days are hectic.

The holiday season is often the most stressful time of the year, as costs and time must be balanced with providing "perfect" gifts for friends and family.

But you might want to stop and consider yourself fortunate.

The World Bank recently stated that about half of the world's 6.5 billion people are living on less than $2 a day. That's less than half the price of many people's morning pick-me-up.

This year, share your blessings with others by donating to charity. Even a dollar a day can support a child or provide lifesaving medicine for dozens of people.

Life may be hard, but it's a lot tougher for others. Share your opportunities with needy people in your community and around the world.

The measure you give will be the measure you get, and still more will be given you. (Mark 4:24)

Help me share my advantages with the less fortunate, Lord.

Never Give Up

Former NFL quarterback Danny Wuerffel was devastated when hurricane Katrina laid waste to his hometown of New Orleans.

The entire Ninth Ward was destroyed along with his home. Wuerffel however was most concerned about the 190 students of the Desire Street Academy where he worked as director of development.

Initially he couldn't locate them, but eventually all the students were found. Wuerffel asked his alma mater, the University of Florida, for the use of their Niceville 4-H camp so that classes could continue. Seventy students relocated. Meanwhile Wuerffel is raising funds to restore the Desire Street Academy.

Never give up on a city or its people.

There is hope for a tree, if it is cut down, that it will sprout again...though its root grows old...and its stump dies...yet at the scent of water it will bud and put forth branches like a young plant. (Job 14:7,8)

God, grant that I may never lose hope–in You, in myself, in the persistence of goodness and life.

Stay Strong

To effectively manage times of stress use healthy coping skills, not dubious methods such as excessive eating, drinking or spending.

"There are ways to nurture true inner peace when outer peace isn't an option," writes psychologist Joan Borysenko.

Her tips include trying to make just one thing better and having an emergency plan that helps you feel in control. Borysenko also suggests:

- Stop listening to the same distressing news reports over and over again. "One exposure to mayhem is more than enough."
- Set your internet home page to a site with inspirational stories.
- Learn from the super-resilient who are "optimistic and altruistic, have a moral compass and use humor."
- Explore faith and spirituality. To be resilient you need to have "a sense that life has meaning."

The waves of death encompassed me, the torrents of perdition assailed me; the cords of Sheol entangled me...death confronted me. In my distress...to my God I called.
(2 Samuel 22:5-7)

Holy Spirit, protect us!

The Satisfaction of Being Santa

Tom Hartsfield is Santa Claus. Don't believe him? He'll gladly invite you to tug on his beard.

As founder of the Amalgamated Order of Real Bearded Santas, Hartsfield has made a career of donning the red suit and hat and capturing people's imaginations.

After discovering the beard is real, children give him "sort of a shocked look," Hartsfield says. "The real beard makes them believe more."

He believes that the decision to become a Kris Kringle look-alike is monumental, since one's entire appearance must be altered. However, the passion for spreading joy and being able to see children's excitement makes it all worthwhile.

Such simple pleasures have enticed thousands of Santas around the world into this jolly, merry way of life.

How will you spread joy to others today?

Do not neglect to do good. (Hebrews 13:16)

Help me share my love with everyone, generous Lord.

Resting on the Seventh Day

God "blessed the seventh day and hallowed it, because on it God rested." (Genesis 2:3) Through the ages humans have tried to keep a day of rest, a Sabbath.

Teacher Mike Daley, writing in the *National Catholic Reporter,* adds another reason for keeping days of complete rest when he quotes Voltaire, "If you want to kill the human person, abolish the Sabbath."

Daley then describes a snow day when his son Brendan pulled him away from grading papers and planning lessons. They bundled up, shoveled the driveway, sledded and played in the snow. Instead of being consumed by work and activity, Daley opened himself "to the present moment...to just having fun."

That's all the more reason to take a weekly day of rest as well as an annual vacation. We are God's well-loved daughters and sons, not profit-centers or machines.

**Thus says the Lord: For the sake of your lives, take care that you...keep the Sabbath day holy, as I commanded your ancestors.
(Jeremiah 17:21,22)**

Give us the fortitude and wisdom to keep weekly days and annual times of complete rest, God of the Sabbath.

Hope...Miracle...Joy

The word "miracle" can conjure up many beautiful thoughts. Many of us may have seen, heard or even witnessed a miracle at some time. But what is it that brings about these miracles? Is it the hand of God? Fate? Coincidence?

A little girl who had leukemia wanted to meet Santa before she died. The Santa at the local mall heard about her and paid her a visit. Needless to say, the girl's joy knew no bounds. Then Santa gave her a rare gift...the gift of hope. He told her to concentrate on getting well, to enjoy summer and to visit him next Christmas.

One year later, the girl could be found sitting on Santa's lap, cheerful and well.

As Bernard Berenson said, "Miracles happen to those who believe"—and they go hand in hand with hope and joy.

(Jesus) said..."If you have faith the size of a mustard seed...nothing will be impossible for you." (Matthew 17:20)

Merciful Father, increase my faith! And may Your will be done in me.

Anna Okot, Courageous Woman

For more than twenty years war has raged in northern Uganda. Anna Okot and her six children are among the many displaced families. "When I came from my home, I had nothing," she says.

At a displaced persons camp, Okot planted, harvested and sold crops: beans netted $30 for household items; tomatoes, $12 for a goat; cabbages, a small radio; cowpeas, her children's school fees.

Okot knows that "when families are displaced by war, women cannot rebuild by themselves. We need to work together to earn money." She helped form *Lacan Kwitte* (A Poor Person Struggles). The women members get seeds, tools, and cows for plowing; and are trained in small-scale savings, loan management and leadership skills.

Poor women around the world struggle to live independently and productively and to support their families. How can we help?

My wife Anna earned money at women's work...One day...when she cut off a piece she had woven...they paid her full wages and also gave her a young goat. (Tobit 2:11,12)

Holy God, Anna, the wife of the blind Tobit, supported them both by weaving cloth. Show us how to assist poor women.

Meaningful Christmas Gifts

Having a hard time finding that perfect gift for someone? How about doing something different this year? *Today's Christian Woman* lists some alternatives to common Christmas gifts.

- Frame a copy of your favorite Scripture verse, quotation, or poem. Words that mean something to you can mean as much to someone else.

- Gather five or ten of your favorite recipes into a journal. Write why you liked these particular dishes so much.

- Create personalized coupon books for activities like a backrub, overnight trip, breakfast in bed, bedtime stories, and more.

- Give someone a book you enjoyed and tell them why you liked it so much.

Thoughtful gifts don't have to cost lots of money. Personalizing a present from your heart is a great way to connect with another person at the Christmas season.

A generous person will be enriched.
(Proverbs 11:25)

Show me how to be generous yet practical, Holy Spirit.

Unconditional Compassion

During World War II, there was a prisoner of war camp in Houlton, Maine. German POWs, filling in for local men fighting overseas, were treated with respect and compassion by most of the citizens. Here are a few examples:

Catherine Bell treated each POW with the same dignity as the other workers on her potato farm. Sixty years later, one went with her to visit her soldier brother's grave in Europe.

Farmer Fenton Shaw and his wife Eve gave extra food to the prisoners in the field and also ate with them to ease concerns about the food's safety. After the war, Shaw received a package of German dolls, candies, and gifts from some former POWs.

Unconditional compassion is the very hard way of peace.

Blessed are the peacemakers, for they will be called children of God. (Matthew 5:9)

Creator of all, open our eyes to the human cost of war and help us to seek peace in all we say and do.

Have You Looked at Yourself Lately?

Many people go through life thinking that they are right in everything they do or, at least, in everything they believe.

One writer noticed such an attitude in himself when his wife brought him to a marriage counselor. He was skeptical. His first thought when he and his wife went for counseling was that the counselor could really help his wife.

However, he finally understood that he was the one who needed help because he had always given his job priority over his marriage and his family. He realized, "The most important step in embracing the concept of personal responsibility is the willingness to change how you think. Thinking about others first is the ultimate act of personal responsibility."

Take responsibility for your actions. Look at yourself from another's point of view and think about how you can change yourself for the better.

Judge your neighbor's feelings by your own. (Sirach 31:15)

Help married couples realize that each partner is responsible for the health of their relationship, Abba.

Operation Christmas Child to the Rescue

During the Christmas season, many charities give gifts to children who would not otherwise receive any. One of these is Operation Christmas Child, an organization that brings presents in shoeboxes to children overseas.

One of the homes visited by this non-profit was the Dulla family of Vukovar, Croatia. The seven children and their widowed mom still feel the effects of the war that ended a decade ago—including poverty and unemployment. Though Dulla cares for her children to the best of her ability, there's not enough money for Christmas gifts.

But when Operation Christmas Child came knocking on the Dulla family's door, life was full of hope—even for a brief moment. A member of the group recalls, "It's amazing that through a simple shoebox, Jesus can give significance to a child who feels unloved."

Share God's love with those in trouble.

Wise men from the East...saw the Child with Mary His mother; and they knelt down and paid Him homage. Then...they offered Him gifts of gold, frankincense, and myrrh.
(Matthew 2:1,11)

May we share the hope and joy the celebration of Your birthday brings, Infant Jesus.

Lakota Prayers

Consider enriching your spiritual life with meditations from different backgrounds. This prayer, for example, comes from the Lakota Christian tradition:

"Grandfather and Great Spirit, we ask you to give us direction today, and provide for our needs, as you are the One, that understands and knows our needs and You can guide us.

"Today, we pray for those who are mourning, and we ask that You give them comfort. We pray for our deceased relatives that You have given them a place of rest, and that they be happy with their relatives."

"Grandfather and Great Spirit, as we walk through this day, You understand and know everything and we ask for Your protection, blessing, good health and happiness. Help us! And let us not forget our kinship, by loving each other in our daily walk in life."

However you pray, pray always.

I am the Lord...besides Me there is no god. (Isaiah 45:5)

Father, prosper and protect all Your people, everywhere.

Painting a Perfect Ending

Visual artist Michael Landis, who has had type-1 diabetes since age six, is no stranger to health problems. After being hospitalized with pneumonia and acute renal failure, his body was at permanent risk.

Landis could not paint a more perfect picture of what happened next: he received a kidney transplant–from his upstairs neighbor.

Tom Abbs, who was both his neighbor and artistic collaborator, jumped at the opportunity to help Landis after learning he was an almost perfect match.

"His generosity goes beyond words," said Landis. "Tom kept telling me, 'We've done so many collaborations, let's consider this our next one'," Landis said. "I've already gotten way more than a Christmas present," Landis added. "I've gotten a life present."

The help you need may be right next to you. Extend your love to your neighbors and all those around you.

Love your neighbor as yourself. (Mark 12:31)

Open our hearts to all with whom we share Your world, Creator.

Primates and Morals

While ethical behavior is generally considered exclusively human, some scientists believe that certain primates exhibit moral actions. Primatologist Frans de Waal is one of them.

He believes that Bonobos and chimpanzees are capable of a certain amount of ethical behavior.

"If people commit mass murder, we call them 'animals,'" de Waal says. "But if they give money to the poor, we praise them for their 'humanity.'"

He says that his research shows that these primates express not only feelings like fear, rage and territorial instincts, but higher emotions such as justice and sympathy. Bononos are remarkably friendly and sociable creatures while chimpanzees share food and exhibit shame, guilt and concern.

Whatever abilities other creatures may or may not have, we humans have an obligation to lead moral lives.

God said, "Let the waters bring forth swarms of living creatures, and let birds fly above the earth...Let the earth bring forth living creatures of every kind: cattle and creeping things and wild animals. (Genesis 1:20,24)

Divine Master, imbue us with a whole-souled respect for all Your creatures.

Give Me Patience!

It's easy to become frustrated during the holidays with too much to do in too little time. Whether you're stuck in a long shopping line or rushing to finish your to-do list, patience is a virtue that will help you overcome these situations without stress.

"Patience is about compassion and acceptance, qualities that benefit all of us as a community," says M.J. Ryan, author of *The Power of Patience*.

The idea is to put things into perspective. Will the extra minute of waiting for a cashier who is slow in handing you change really affect your life that much? Is a minor inconvenience really worth the stress and anger?

"Every time you practice patience, it really does help change you and the way you operate in the world," adds Ryan.

How will you practice patience this season?

**Endure everything with patience.
(Colossians 1:11)**

Merciful Savior, help me to be patient with myself and with others—loved ones and strangers alike.

Santa's Big Helpers

Writing a letter to Santa Claus is one thing that children the world over love to do. But receiving a letter from Santa Claus would really be special. Where could such a letter come from? Well, it would help if you know about a town named Santa Claus.

Santa Claus, Indiana, has a population of just over 2,000. The number of letters the town receives crosses the 15,000 mark every year. Its inhabitants spend their Christmases replying to these letters from children across the globe. This volunteer effort is a town tradition.

What do they get out of it? Nothing but the feeling of satisfaction that a child somewhere is filled with joy as he or she clutches a letter from Santa Claus in his or her hand. To do something and expect nothing in return...now that's a beautiful deed!

Do good...expecting nothing in return. Your reward will be great, and you will be children of the Most High. (Luke 6:36)

Remind us, Child Jesus, that children need loving attention from their parents and their good neighbors.

Better to Give?

One December, Peter McFadden was almost broke and sleeping in his Washington office. The non-profit organization he'd started in Prague, Czech Republic, to help entrepreneurs start small businesses was near bankruptcy. He also faced a mountain of government forms and the unbearable thought of going home without Christmas presents.

Walking near-midnight, he passed an old man huddled on a doorstep. McFadden asked him, "Excuse me sir, but do you have a place to stay?" The homeless man named Robert had been thinking about suicide. Instead, Robert slept on McFadden's couch and ate dinner with him for the next few days.

On the day after Christmas, McFadden found a church shelter for Robert. That same day he was notified that he'd been awarded a $50,000 grant to continue his non-profit.

Did one have anything to do with the other? Perhaps not, but Peter McFadden says simply, "I thank God for my wonderful life."

Share your bread with the hungry, and bring the homeless poor into your house.
(Isaiah 58:7)

Christ, open our eyes to You in a homeless, friendless stranger's guise.

Brighten Someone's Day

Susan Fawcett worked at a post office and was getting tired of standing and helping people for so many hours. Then the Christmas season arrived and work was even harder.

Fawcett's mood changed when an elderly woman came to the window. The woman had received a package from her grandchild who only included the street name without a number—and instead of her name had simply put "Granny." The woman wanted to thank the post office for delivering this special package. Fawcett called the woman's mail carrier, so she could personally thank him as well. This woman made Fawcett's day—and all she did was say "thank you."

Expressing gratitude to service industry workers for something they have done can give them a real boost. The simplest act of courtesy or appreciation can brighten someone's day.

**A gracious tongue multiplies courtesies.
(Sirach 6:5)**

Enable us to be respectful and gracious at all times and in all circumstances, God who respects us and is gracious to us in all ways and at all times.

A Debt of Charity

Imagine walking down the street and being stopped by a stranger. The stranger hands you a $100 bill, wishes you a Merry Christmas, and walks away! Larry Stewart has made this unlikely situation a reality for almost 30 years.

Born and raised in poverty, Stewart often had to rely on others for food, money, and hope. Depending on the support of others, he was able to start a multi-million dollar business and earn a good living for himself.

Then Stewart decided to devote himself to helping others as a way to return the compassion he'd known when he was in need. Dubbed "Secret Santa" by the media for his original insistence on anonymity, Stewart estimates he's doled out more than $1.3 million in Christmas money.

How can you extend yourself with generosity? Through money? Time? Talent? Think about it.

Be rich in good works, generous.
(1 Timothy 6:18)

Show me how to be grateful and generous, Father.

Passing Through

In the 18th century, the renowned Polish rabbi, Hofetz Chaim, had a visitor who was astounded that the rabbi's home was only a simple room filled with books, a table and a bench.

"Rabbi, where is your furniture?" the visitor asked.

"Where is yours?" asked Rabbi Chaim.

"Mine? But I'm only a visitor here. I'm only passing through," the man replied.

"So am I," said the rabbi.

It's easy to forget that even if we live to be a hundred, our stay on this earth is brief. Deciding on the really important things in life also means deciding what's not important. Trying to simplify our lives can be hard. We tend to accumulate things, even when they are not necessary.

But it's easier to let go of the extraneous things if we trust that God will give us all we really need.

Do not worry, saying, 'What will we eat?... drink?...wear?'...Your heavenly Father knows that you need all these things. But strive first for the kingdom of God and His righteousness. (Matthew 6:31,32-33)

Merciful God, help me examine my life and eliminate everything that comes between us.

Dreaming of a Hit

I'm dreaming of a White Christmas/Just like the ones I used to know...

These are lyrics from the number one Christmas song and the number one selling single of all-time. Surprisingly, at first *White Christmas* didn't impress anyone except its composer.

Calling it "the best song anybody ever wrote," Irving Berlin needed a vehicle to launch the song. He pushed it everywhere, finally approaching Bing Crosby. Crosby failed to see its promise, but reluctantly agreed to sing it in the movie *Holiday Inn.*

Reviewers barely noticed until troops overseas in WWII asked Crosby to sing it during USO performances. The song reminded them of home and family.

After that, it made history. The song has since been recorded by over 150 performers. Not bad for a song that almost never was.

Entrust your creativity and dreams to God.

(Jacob) dreamed that...the Lord stood beside him and said...the land on which you lie I will give to you and to your offspring.
(Genesis 28:12,13)

Remind me, Holy Spirit, that my dreams are only limited by the strength of my convictions—and my reliance on You.

The Ultimate Christmas Gift

Assigned to a run-down church in Brooklyn, a newly-ordained pastor and his wife did what they could to fix it up.

With Christmas Eve approaching and the repairs nearly complete, a storm put a hole in the church's roof. Not wanting to cancel services, the pastor bought a colorful tablecloth from a local flea market to cover the hole.

While he was arranging the cloth, a woman told him she recognized it as one she made before fleeing the Nazis in Austria. She had escaped, but never saw her husband or home again.

That night at services, the pastor noticed an elderly man staring at the same cloth. Later he recounted the tale of how his wife had made one just like it before escaping the Nazis.

That Christmas a married couple was reunited and a sense of faith was renewed. Perhaps that's the ultimate Christmas gift.

A child has been born for us, a son given to us; authority rests upon his shoulders; and he is named Wonderful Counselor, Mighty God, Everlasting Father, Prince of Peace. (Isaiah 9:6)

May we find Your Son when and where we least expect Him, Father.

A Christmas Prayer

Robert Louis Stevenson, the famous 19th century Scottish lawyer, poet and author, wrote this lovely *Christmas Prayer.*

"O God, our loving Father, help us rightly to remember the birth of Jesus, that we may share in the song of the angels, the gladness of the shepherds, and the worship of the wise men.

"Close the door of hate and open the door of love all over the world.

"Deliver us from evil by the blessing that Christ brings, and teach us to be merry with clear hearts. May the Christmas morning make us happy to be Thy children and the Christmas Evening bring us to our beds with grateful thoughts, forgiving, and forgiven, for Jesus' sake. Amen."

Yes, dearest Abba, please "close the door of hate and open the door of love" for all of us, Your children.

Joseph, son of David, do not be afraid to take Mary as your wife...She will bear a son, and you are to name him Jesus, for He will save His people from their sins. (Matthew 1:20-21)

Thank You, God, for all those who bring Your peace and love to their little patch of this earth of ours and Yours.

A Moment of Realization

The Sudan has been plagued by ethnic cleansing, mass murder, looting and rape. Women and children have been enslaved. The humanitarian relief agency Christian Solidarity International (CSI) is trying to free the enslaved and to provide the Sudanese Dinka people with food and medicine.

Photographer Lucien Niemeyer joined CSI, asking himself: "What am I doing here? What can I do to relieve this sorrow?" At the same time, Niemeyer had experienced in the Sudan a heartfelt fulfillment that he had not anticipated.

When he took pictures he realized that God had sent him to bear witness – to show others the suffering of God's children and the goodness that can survive even tragedy.

God gives each of us talents. Do we permit God to use the talent He's given us for His purposes?

Woe to you who strive with your Maker, earthen vessels with the potter! Does the clay say to the one who fashions it, "What are you making?" (Isaiah 45:9)

Divine Potter, I desire to let You use the gifts You've given me as You would. Give me the needed courage.

"The Good Old Days"

There are two ways to age.

Optimistically: You and your spouse have health concerns, but medical care is improving. The children are doing OK. Communication and travel are easier; the media, more alert. The world's problems are more out in the open. More people are becoming tolerant.

It's good just to breathe, to feel, to see and be seen, to laugh and cry, to embrace and be embraced. What a wonderful time to be alive!

Pessimistically: You and your spouse are sick and you fear what tomorrow may bring. The children are not fulfilling *your* expectations. Communication and travel are complex. The media exposes insuperable problems. People question authority; are less courteous and less moral than in the good old days.

Truth be told, "the good old days" never existed. Human memory is selective. Choose optimism; choose life!

Fear God and keep His commandments. (Ecclesiastes 12:13)

Holy Spirit, help us to embrace the present and future with optimism and enthusiasm instead of dwelling on the past.

The Accidental Historian

Although Aaron Lansky was merely exploring a personal interest when he began to research the history and use of Yiddish, he contributed to the revival and preservation of the language.

Lansky grew up in New York City where Yiddish was common in some neighborhoods. Derived from Hebrew, German, French, Italian and Slavic and written in Hebrew characters, Yiddish dates back more than 1,000 years. Roughly a century ago, it was the first or only language of 80 percent of the world's Jews.

Lansky began collecting books on Yiddish and found a wealth of history and culture. "Hebrew traditionally was the language of scholarship and prayer, while Yiddish was the language of everyday life," he explains. His book, *Outwitting History,* helped reignite interest in Yiddish among Jews and non-Jews alike.

Each language and each culture has a rich tradition. Seek to understand and appreciate them.

Do not speak evil against one another....Who, then, are you to judge your neighbor? (James 4:11-12)

Teach us respect for our unique selves and our culture, then of others' unique selves and their cultures, Father Creator.

Happily Married: the Next Generation

Parents want the best for their youngsters, including a happy adulthood, which usually means marriage. There are ways they can improve their children's chances for wedded bliss.

Nancy Darling, associate professor of psychology at Oberlin College in Ohio, did a study which found that modeling a good marriage is not enough. The parent-child relationship itself makes a huge difference. Here are three ways to help youngsters:

- Argue rationally. Teach conflict-resolution skills. They'll know how to handle problems as adults.

- Be supportive. Set limits. They'll expect friends and partners who will look out for them, too.

- Set boundaries about where and how your children make friends. They'll be more likely to meet "good kids."

Children need the very best their parents can give them. Now—and later.

Honor your father and your mother, so that your days may be long in the land that the Lord your God is giving you. (Exodus 20:12)

Loving God, bless all parents. Encourage them to guide their children well.

Pain with a Purpose

When Cindy La Ferle was diagnosed with severe osteoarthritis at just 44 years of age, she began a vigorous search for guidance on coping with chronic illness and its pain.

She was amazed at how many times she'd encounter the suggestion, "Look for the gift in your pain." Cindy's immediate reaction was, "Pain as a gift? Are you kidding?"

When her disease rendered her immobile, she became reclusive, a reaction her loved ones wouldn't tolerate. Then, through her friends' and family's persistence, came the "gift" of pain: she realized that chronic illness had opened her to others' boundless love and generosity.

At a time when society exalts unrealistic perfection as an ultimate ideal, it's not easy to show vulnerability. But by accepting our flaws and struggles, we grow closer to God and become more of our true selves.

My grace is sufficient for you, for power is made perfect in weakness.
(2 Corinthians 12:9)

Jesus, Your very existence teaches us that when we are weak, we are indeed strong.

How to Be Perfectly Miserable

If you want to be sure that you have a sad, unhappy life, then follow these "tips" from *Gospel Herald:*

- Talk about yourself.
- Use "I" as often as possible.
- Listen to what others say about you.
- Expect to be appreciated.
- Be suspicious, jealous and envious.
- Never forgive a criticism.
- Never forget a service you've rendered.
- Shirk your duties.
- Do as little as possible for others.
- Love yourself supremely.

If, on the other hand, you'd like to be happy, aim for the opposite. Without neglecting your own needs, live the Golden Rule: Do unto others as you would have them do unto you.

You shall love your neighbor as yourself: I am the Lord. (Leviticus 19:18)

Show me how to truly love myself and others, in Your love, with Your love, for Your love, my Lord and my God.

Also Available

Have you enjoyed volume 42 of *Three Minutes a Day*? These other Christopher offerings may interest you:

- **News Notes** – published 10 times a year on a variety of topics of current interest. One copy as published is free; quantity orders available.

- **Ecos Cristóforos** – Spanish translations of selected News Notes. Issued six times a year. One copy as published is free; quantity orders available.

- **Wall or Desk Appointment Calendar** – The Calendar offers an inspirational message for each day.

- **Videocassettes** – Christopher videos range from wholesome entertainment to serious discussions of family life and current social and spiritual issues.

For more information on The Christophers or to receive **News Notes, Ecos Cristóforos** or a catalogue:

The Christophers
5 Hanover Square, 11th Floor
New York, NY 10004
Phone: 212-759-4050 / 888-298-4050
E-mail: mail@christophers.org
Website: www.christophers.org

The Christophers is a non-profit media organization founded in 1945. We share the message of personal responsibility and service to God and humanity with people of all faiths and no particular faith. Gifts are welcome and tax-deductible. Our legal title for wills is The Christophers, Inc.